slaughter
of the
innocents

Jossey-Bass Inc., Publishers
615 Montgomery Street • San Francisco • 1971

SLAUGHTER OF THE INNOCENTS
A Study of the Battered Child Phenomenon
    David Bakan

The poem "Boy," from *This Strangest Everything* by John Ciardi (copyright
1966 by Rutgers, The State University), reprinted by permission of the author.

The Jossey-Bass
Behavioral Science Series

General Editors

WILLIAM E. HENRY, University of Chicago

NEVITT SANFORD, Wright Institute, Berkeley

To All Parents and All Children,
But Especially to Those Who Are
Both Parents and Children

Preface

The thought presented in *Slaughter of the Innocents* is an extension of considerations developed in earlier books, *The Duality of Human Existence*[1] and *Disease, Pain and Sacrifice*.[2] One of my main purposes has been to combine considerations of "ultimate concern," as Paul Tillich characterized religious concern, with what we have learned about people through modern empirical and rational methods. I have long been troubled by what has sometimes seemed to be an inevitable inverse relationship between the importance of the psychologist's subject matter and his ability to make sense out of it in ways consistent with the canons of commonly accepted methods. In *The Duality of Human Existence* I developed two concepts which I called agency and communion. If I may take the liberty of quoting my own words:

[1] D. Bakan, *The Duality of Human Existence* (Chicago: Rand McNally, 1966).
[2] D. Bakan, *Disease, Pain and Sacrifice* (Chicago: University of Chicago Press, 1968).

Preface

I have adopted the terms "agency" and "communion" to characterize two fundamental modalities in the existence of living forms, agency for the existence of an organism as an individual, and communion for the participation of the individual in some larger organism of which the individual is a part. Agency manifests itself in self-protection, self-assertion, and self-expansion; communion manifests itself in the sense of being at one with other organisms. Agency manifests itself in the formation of separations; communion in the lack of separations. Agency manifests itself in isolation, alienation, and aloneness; communion in contact, openness, and union. Agency manifests itself in the urge to master; communion in noncontractual cooperation. Agency manifests itself in the repression of thought, feeling, and impulse; communion in the lack and removal of repression.[3]

Informed by the cosmic significance attributed to sex in the Jewish mystical tradition and the psychological significance attributed to sex in psychoanalysis, and searching for empirical touchstones to make my meanings explicit, I reviewed the empirical literature on sexuality and sex differences. I found that I could round out my meanings of agency and communion by assuming that which was more characteristic of males as agentic and that which was more characteristic of females as communal, although always recognizing the essential bisexuality of both males and females. I took the ideal of human existence to be the integration of agency and communion and the conspicuous paradigm of that integration to be the human family. In the family we have the integration of agency and communion between individuals working toward the integration of agency and communion within individuals, the creation of new life, caring for it into adulthood, and guaranteeing a chance for the only kind of immortality that is both physically and spiritually possible.

[3] Bakan, *The Duality of Human Existence*, pp. 14–15.

If the man-woman-child "holy trinity" is a kind of ultimate paradigm of wholeness, wholesomeness, and holiness, what then corresponds to sin? I came to believe that the answer must be infanticide, the killing of the new life that results from the coming together of the male and the female. The crushing out of the life of a child is, in my opinion, the most heinous of all crimes.

When I was a child I was told that the story of the fall of man had a hidden secret: the fruit of the tree of knowledge which Adam and Eve ate was a baby. I failed to understand it at the time. However, the biblical writers use the same word for knowing and sexual intercourse, and thus they may indeed have intended to tell us that the fruit of knowledge is an infant. This interpretation was transmitted to me orally, and I suspect that it arises out of a long oral tradition. The dawn of civilization must have been when man learned that through planting seed, in the ground or sexually, he could create life at will. According to Charles Darwin, the beginning of civilization was associated with infanticide: "Our early semi-human progenitors would not have practiced infanticide, . . . for the instincts of the lower animals are never so perverted as to lead them regularly to destroy their own offspring."[4] In Roman law the two acts of will, creating the child and extinguishing the life of the child, became united, with the former providing the license for the latter.[5] A writer in the *Spectator* of March 12, 1871, in commenting on Darwin's dating the onset of civilization from the onset of infanticide, indicated that Darwin was indeed making a suggestion concerning the meaning of the story of the fall of man, providing for it a "new doctrine."[6]

The development of cognitive interest is a mystery.

---

[4] C. Darwin, *The Origin of Species* and *The Descent of Man* (New York: Modern Library, 1936), p. 430.

[5] See R. W. Lee, *The Elements of Roman Law* (4th ed.) (London: Sweet and Maxwell, 1956).

[6] Darwin, p. 430.

Yet a cognitive process informed by considerations such as these brought me to ask what in the contemporary world may enter into a dialectical process with these ideas, enrich them, and perhaps be enriched by them. The answer came with eminent clarity. What about the problem of child abuse, which has been coming to public attention? *Slaughter of the Innocents* is the result.

The genius of the twentieth century is related to its resolve to pursue truth relentlessly. The mind of the twentieth century, the century of psychoanalysis on the one hand and the Nazi concentration camps on the other, appreciates that virtue is not served by not looking at evil. Quite the opposite —the refusal to face evil serves to perpetuate it. The moral imperative that emerges is to examine evil closely. The reader will not find this a pleasant book. I only hope that it may increase our understanding of and help to remove the evil that it speaks of.

The material in *Slaughter of the Innocents* is a somewhat extended and amended version of a series of five radio talks that I gave for the Canadian Broadcasting Corporation. I would like to express my appreciation to Janet Somerville, who produced the first four of the programs, to Lou Auerbach, who produced the fifth, and to Phyllis Webb, director of *Ideas,* the series in which the programs were broadcast. I am especially grateful to them for helping me to overcome my own resistance to discussing these ideas publicly. Indeed, it still remains in the nature of what I have to say that it would be better to talk about these matters in intimate conversation, where at least one may easily recognize and respond to uneasinesses and misunderstandings. Yet, having presented these ideas on the air with no dire consequences, I find myself with the courage to present them in written form.

Toronto   DAVID BAKAN
February 1971

Contents

Slaughter of the Innocents

A Study of the
Battered Child Phenomenon

BOY

He is in his room sulked shut. The small
pouts of his face clenched. His tears
as close to holy water as I recall
any first font shining. A boy, and fierce
in his sacrament, father-forced this two-
faced way love has. And I, who

am chain-chafed and galled as any son,
his jailor: my will, his cell;
his hot eyes, mine. "Whose will be done?"
I think, wrong as a man. —Oh, very well:
I make too much of nothing much. My
will a while. A boy's tears dry

into the smudge of any jam. Time hurts,
but I am not much destiny. I am,
at best, what cries with him; at worst,
a smallest God, the keeper of one lamb
that must be made to follow. —Where?
That takes more God than I am to make clear.

I'm wrong as a man is. But right as love,
and father of the man whose tears I bless
in this bud boy. May he have cried enough
when he has cried this little. I confess
I don't know my own reasons or own way.
May sons forgive the fathers they obey.

From *This Strangest Everything*
John Ciardi

ONE

ᘰᘰᘰᘰᘰᘰᘰᘰᘰᘰᘰᘰᘰᘰᘰᘰᘰ

Looking
the Other Way

ᘰᘰᘰᘰᘰᘰᘰᘰᘰᘰᘰᘰᘰᘰᘰᘰᘰ

It has now become an open secret that people torture and kill their own children or children in their charge. But prior to recent publicity there was a virtual blackout, reaching far back into history, on the topic. Statements here and there in the literature indicate to a knowing eye conditions of child abuse. However, the written history of our civilization shows much less than the magnitude of the problem, which we can assume to have been serious. The problem did not start just a few years ago when a group of physicians found the courage to make public notice of it. The very delay of public recognition of the phenomenon is to be wondered at as one wonders about the phenomenon itself.

A consideration of the past silence and of its recent removal may in itself help us to unlock some of the mystery. I hypothesize here that the essential functions of child abuse are in the area of adaptations to population-resource[1] balance. The abused child may die. If he lives he tends to make reduced claims on the available resources. If he grows up he becomes an adult less likely to reproduce. If he reproduces, he is likely to abuse children in turn. If this hypothesis be true, then, as child abuse served its harsh function in history, it had to stay hidden under the cloak of silence. The community, in its way, assented to the phenomenon simply because it could not afford to do otherwise.

Why can the veil of silence be lifted now? The answer lies in the fantastic increase in the level and role of technology in our lives in modern times. Technology has made three contributions. First, and most concretely, the technology of the X-ray plate provided objective evidence of child abuse to supplement all human testimony by showing fractures in the bones of babies at different stages of healing. These fractures indicate successive instances of trauma that accident can hardly explain. Second, technology has provided great advances in resource provision. Third, technology has provided promises of acceptable and humane population control. It is therefore now possible to apprehend the ugly and odious adjustment to the population-resource balance that child abuse represents in a way that has not been possible before.

If one cannot comfortably pretend that the abuse of children does not take place, one is at least tempted to pretend that it must be rare or limited to persons with frank mental disturbance. Unfortunately it is not rare. And, furthermore, unless one wishes to take the very fact of abusive

---

[1] Resource here means both goods and services. The latter especially is intended to include direct and indirect child-care services.

2

behavior as evidence of frank mental disturbance, the mental disturbance hypothesis is not supported by fact.

If one decides to behold what has been thus avoided, one becomes possessed of an anguished "Why?" Why do they do it? How can anyone torture and even kill a child? Evil always compromises us. We stand in horror before it and demand that it explain itself. But should plausible and credible explanation be forthcoming, it frightens us also. Explanation can function as excuse; and when the evil is so monstrous we do not tolerate the possibility that it is excusable. We cannot overcome the forgiveness that understanding tends to produce, and thus we are loath to try to understand. The task of this book is nonetheless to try to understand child abuse. It is not to condone it. The history of child abuse indicates that the very abstention from deliberate concern with it has played a role in perpetuating it. Child abuse thrives in the shadows of privacy and secrecy. It lives by inattention. Those who have protected themselves from being witness to it have at the same time protected the practice and have thus been a party to it.

I look at the phenomenon from different perspectives. Some of what I say is frankly speculative. I am fully aware of the tenuousness of some of the considerations that I set forth. I venture my main hypothesis, that child abuse is an evolutionary mechanism associated with population-resource balance, with some misgivings. It may not be valid. But that is the lesser of my misgivings. Beyond that, I fear the suggestion that such a hypothesis may provoke—that the abuse of children should be regarded as "natural" and therefore not subject to deliberate modification. My belief is rather that the contrary suggestion should emerge: by man's comprehension of what is natural he is placed in a position to make modifications. This has been the paradoxical history of man's conquest of nature. As his understanding of the forces of nature has increased, his ability to make things happen

3

in accordance with his values and his will has also increased. The social Darwinist, who interpreted Charles Darwin's contribution to biology as an excuse for social neglect, was guilty of the logical fallacy of confusing the descriptive with the normative, the "is" with the "ought." Men have always sought to understand nature, not for the purpose of leaving circumstances unmanaged but to learn how to manage them.

OCCURRENCE OF CHILD ABUSE

In numerous known and publicly recorded instances children have been victimized by those responsible for their care. Children have been brought into hospitals with skulls fractured and bodies covered with lacerations. One parent disciplined a child for presumptive misbehavior with the buckle end of a belt, perforating an intestine and killing the child. Children have been whipped, beaten, starved, drowned, smashed against walls and floors, held in ice water baths, exposed to extremes of outdoor temperatures, burned with hot irons and steam pipes. Children have been tied and kept in upright positions for long periods. They have been systematically exposed to electric shock; forced to swallow pepper, soil, feces, urine, vinegar, alcohol, and other odious materials; buried alive; had scalding water poured over their genitals; had their limbs held in open fire; placed in roadways where automobiles would run over them; placed on roofs and fire escapes in such a manner as to fall off; bitten, knifed, and shot; had their eyes gouged out. "The reports of injuries read like the case book of the concentration camp doctor," says a reporter.[2]

Are these events of great rarity? How prevalent can such occurrences be? Clearly data are hard to come by because in only the most extreme cases do such things come to public notice. Yet available information strongly suggests

[2] C. Flato, "Parents Who Beat Children," *Saturday Evening Post*, 1962, *235*, 30.

4

that the frequency is far greater than one may naively, or hopefully, imagine.

A questionnaire sent to all 715 physicians of the Hawaii Medical Association inquired of their experiences with child abuse. Of the 393 physicians who responded, forty-four reported that they had seen children who had been abused in the preceding twelve-month period. Ten of these physicians were in pediatrics, eighteen were in general practice, and the remainder were distributed among other specialties. Thus, more than 11 per cent of those who replied and more than 6 per cent of all physicians in the Hawaii Medical Association witnessed cases of child abuse in a year. Even if we were to assume that all the physicians who failed to answer did not see such cases and even if more than one physician were reporting on the same case, the figures suggest that we are dealing with a major social problem.[3]

Eustace Chesser, studying child abuse in England, concluded that between 6 and 7 per cent of all children are "so neglected or ill-treated or become so maladjusted" as to come to the attention of the National Society for the Prevention of Cruelty to Children.[4] In 1964, twenty thousand children in California were identified as needing protective services.[5] According to one estimate at least 200,000 to 250,000 children in the United States need such services each year. Of these, 30,000 to 37,500 require protection against serious physical abuse.[6]

Figures based on cases which have been brought to the attention of agencies or officials represent only a fraction of all instances of abuse. Available data are systematically

[3] P. H. Patterson and D. Char, "Child Abuse in Hawaii," *Hawaii Medical Journal*, 1966, *25*, 395–397.

[4] E. Chesser, *Cruelty to Children* (New York: Philosophical Library, 1952).

[5] *Planning for the Protection and Care of Neglected Children in California* (Sacramento, Calif.: National Study Service, 1964).

[6] S. R. Zalba, "The Abused Child. I. A Survey of the Problem," *Social Work*, 1966, *11* (4), 8.

5

biased in that the victims are young and mute. One writer comments on those who do not come to the attention of authorities: "What of thousands of tots, with weals physical and mental, whom frightened, bribed, callous, drunken, apathetic neighbours have not mentioned to the police or anyone else? What of hundreds of thousands of children, over a few years, who, left all alone, have pleaded for mercy but have been recklessly assaulted or thrashed by mothers in a temper with their spouse or at emotional loggerheads with husband or man-friend?"[7] Some evidence suggests that most abused children are under three, the largest part being the group under one, and a substantial portion of these being under six months.

INHIBITIONS TO FACING THE PROBLEM

Typically, the abused child has no advocate, no one to take his part against his parents. He is handicapped by his physical and mental immaturity and by what has been the classical legal position of a child with respect to his parents. He is too weak to defend himself against assault. He cannot speak on his own behalf because he has not yet learned how to speak at all. If he were able to speak, hardly anyone would listen. If they listened, they would not believe. If they believed, they would tend to say that the matter was not their business. And if they decided to make it their business, they would find the legal support for their position questionable.

It seems as though we are unable to face not only the problem of child abuse but the topic of cruelty in general. Cruelty is rarely dealt with in nonfiction, although the theme occurs frequently in fiction. In fiction the reader is psychodynamically protected precisely because he is aware that it

[7] G. Bilainkin, "Children in Peril," *Contemporary Review*, 1962, *201*, 67–68.

is fiction. He says to himself, "It is only a story, and no one is really being hurt." I have not been able to find *cruelty* in library card catalogs as a subject heading. In the *Encyclopedia Britannica* I find only two entries under the word *cruelty* in the index. One of these is *Cruelty (divorce)* and the other *Cruelty to Animals acts.* The failure to list cruelty among common bibliographic subject indices speaks loudly in its silence.

A lesson can be learned about the relation of such lack of thought on the topic and the inaction which is the result from the experience of the German concentration camps. Deliberate cruelty was practiced in those camps on the largest scale in history, yet most of the adult Germans of that time appeared to be unaware of what was happening. I do not intend to deal with that history in any detail. Nonetheless I have to agree with one writer who, in discussing the reluctance of the people in England to take cognizance of the extent and degree of child abuse in that country, comments, "Is there not here a symbolic resemblance with the people who pleaded they did not know of Belsen?"[8] And we must also agree with a writer who, in discussing Adolf Eichmann, suggested that the mechanisms associated with Eichmann's evil-doing may be more ubiquitous than commonly supposed: "We do not, of course, identify ourselves as mass killers because we cannot imagine ourselves doing the killing; and this brings us to the crux of the problem: the great crimes of history are often the consequences of a failure of the imagination. . . . Our reluctance to use imagination is often half deliberate."[9]

What, then, is the source of our reluctance to face the problem of child abuse? I suggest that it is because the abuse of a child is repugnant and so also is the abused child

[8] Bilainkin, p. 70.
[9] *New Statesman*, 1961, *61,* 569.

—a fact itself important to my hypothesis. Resistance and defense against facing child abuse is understandable when we recall that one of the major observations of modern psychology is the tendency to push the repugnant out of consciousness. As this is the case in individual psychology, so is it equally the case in society as a whole. The tendency to repress the repugnant is psychodynamically based in part on the failure to distinguish between thought and action. The individual represses thoughts in order to prevent himself from engaging in actions which he takes to be reprehensible. The repression of the reprehensible thought is intended as a way of repressing the reprehensible act. One of the devices available to a therapist is to point out that reprehensible thoughts are not reprehensible actions, and moreover giving reprehensible thoughts an opportunity to be expressed prevents reprehensible acts from becoming actual. We must not allow our abhorrence of an act to become the abhorrence of conscious and deliberate thought and observation in connection with child abuse. Evil is not diminished by not allowing oneself to behold it. The solipsist and the ostrich are wrong, as all sensible people know them to be. Averting one's glance from evil helps it to flourish. On the concrete level, the very emotional reaction that a bystander has to child abuse, an emotion based on a sense of the evil of what he is beholding, brings the bystander into conspiracy with the abuser.

There is unfortunately a close relationship between the characteristic abhorrence that we have toward the abuse of children and the relative absence of research on the question. It is a most remarkable fact that abundant research material on problems of substantially lesser significance exists; but only very recently has scientific entertainment of the problem of child abuse even entered the realm of possibility. Elizabeth Elmer, in commenting on the scantiness of research on the topic, rightly suggests, I believe, that it can be explained by the "taboo . . . regarding abuse and gross neglect. The acute discomfort aroused by the topic leads to extremes of emotion and unquestionably accounts in part for the disregard of the subject by research workers."[10]

It has been observed that indeed the very effort to understand those parents who have tortured their children has the effect of reducing their tendencies to abuse their children.[11] Our progress in finding explanations may be limited. Perhaps no explanation can ever be satisfactory. Perhaps in a matter of this nature explanation must somehow always be of smaller compass than the horrible thing which we entertain in our thoughts. But our very effort at understanding, aside from its ultimate success, itself has direct value. A sage once said that it is not incumbent upon us to complete the whole work, but neither are we free to neglect it. Certainly we must not neglect it as long as there is a child anywhere of whom it may be said, "He is getting it!"

The obligation of society in child abuse cases is not only to try to understand but also to report instances of neglect and abuse. Physicians called upon to treat the injuries of an abused child or to indicate the cause of the death of a child are often placed in compromising positions. Understandably, they have been reluctant to report cases of child abuse. But the temptation is to focus attention on the particular group immediately in contact with any major social problem. Thus, for example, crime rates are often attributed to failures on the part of police when, indeed, the degree and quality of policing is only one factor, and it sometimes can hardly be considered a major factor. A certain amount of attention has been directed toward physicians in connection with child abuse and with their failure to report cases that come to their attention. With the advances that have been made, especially in connection with

[10] E. Elmer, "Identification of Abused Children," *Children*, 1963, *10,* 180.

[11] B. F. Steele and C. B. Pollock, "A Psychiatric Study of Parents Who Abuse Infants and Small Children," in R. E. Helfer and C. H. Kempe, *The Battered Child* (Chicago: University of Chicago Press, 1968), p. 138ff.

9

X rays of the bones in assessing whether child abuse has taken place, the tendency to chide physicians has increased.

One inhibition to reporting, the possibility of retaliatory litigation on the part of the parent, has to a certain degree been handled by the passage of mandatory reporting legislation. However, the possibility of retaliatory litigation is hardly the most important factor associated with the reluctance to report. Here the concrete reality of the role of the physician must be recognized. The existence of child abuse is abhorrent and leads to simple suppression even of what is obvious to the physician. C. Henry Kempe and his colleagues say:

Physicians have great difficulty both in believing that parents could have attacked their children and in undertaking the essential questioning of parents on this subject. Many physicians find it hard to believe that such an attack could have occurred, and they attempt to obliterate such suspicions from their minds, even in the face of obvious circumstantial evidence.[12]

The result of this reaction is that they do nothing. Kempe and his associates suggest that the arousal of the physician's antipathy is so great that it is easier for him to deny what his examination indicates than to deal with the natural anger aroused in him. Thus, the very possibility that the physician would be outraged works paradoxically to make him an accomplice. He is thus led by his emotional reactions to accept the word of the abusing parent against the cogent evidence of his eyes and X-ray plates.

The situation sometimes also places the physician in a position which violates his normal role. Ordinarily, the doctor-patient relationship assumes a patient seeking to be

[12] C. H. Kempe, F. N. Silverman, B. F. Steele, W. Droegenmueller, and H. K. Silver, "The Battered-Child Syndrome," *Journal of the American Medical Association*, 1962, *181*, 107.

helped to overcome disease and pain, and a doctor who will do all he can to help the patient. There is usually no discrepancy in the conscious aim of physician and patient, except with psychiatric patients or very young children who cannot appreciate the nature of their condition. However, the parent-child combination conceived of as a single patient unit introduces problems similar to those of dealing with the suicidal psychiatric patient. A psychiatrist may be prepared to meet a patient whose conscious aim differs from that of the physician. However, the ordinary physician, or certainly the ordinary roentgenologist, is hardly prepared for this. Shirley M. Nurse observes the compromising position in which a physician is placed when he must charge a patient for X rays which may be used as evidence against him.[13] The situation is even more complicated than that involving a suicidal psychiatric patient. In the case of suicide the one who does the killing and the one who may be killed are at least the same person. In the case of child abuse at least two persons are involved, one the victim of the other.

The parent and child as a single unit is quite ordinary in our society, and the physician cannot easily violate the integrity of that unit. He cannot easily, either as a citizen of the society or as a physician, take the role of accuser. In view of the fact that the authority and the responsibility of parenthood are so closely related, anyone would be reluctant to undermine parental authority, even where that authority has been abused. For the physician to do so would be for him to preempt the parental authority and thereby in some sense to arrogate to himself not only the authority but also the parental responsibility with respect to the abused child. In view of these dilemmas of authority and responsibility of individual parents and of collective society, vigorous social action in individual cases is hampered.

[13] S. M. Nurse, "Familial Patterns of Parents Who Abuse Their Children," *Smith College Studies in Social Work*, 1964, *35*, 13.

11

A half-hearted approach in dealing with any single case of child abuse bears the danger that there will be an exacerbation of the condition. This possibility in itself is a reason for being conservative about reporting child abuse cases. To make an accusation against a parent and then still to allow the parent to take responsibility for the child opens the possibility that the child will be savaged in response to the accusation itself.

A final source of difficulty is the wise reluctance of physicians to make diagnoses which suggest heroic therapies. In a case of possible child abuse the conclusion may be uncertain and the outcome even more so.

ROOTS OF REPUGNANCE

As we have seen, repugnance plays an important role in inhibiting action in child abuse cases. Repugnance is dynamically associated with identification, albeit unconscious, with both abuser and victim. In either identification, aspects of ourselves which we would rather not behold are aroused. Child abuse touches each person personally, even if only unconsciously. Every adult was once a child; and every adult is at least potentially responsible for the care of the young for an extremely long part of the total life cycle.

Let us attempt to explicate the nature of these two identifications. First, hardly any adult has not felt at least some twinge of annoyance with a child and has not had some impulse to release his aggression against a child. In our maturity we may hold back our aggression. Yet, from a psychological point of view, the impulse which emerges in such an ugly manner in some is possessed in some measure by many adult persons. Second, we identify with the victim. Each of us has been a child. And while, certainly, each of us has not been the victim of torture, the vision of a child being tortured arouses the sense of weakness and vulnerability that each of us had as a child, together with the empathic pain and fear of death.

12

Consider the first identification. Let us not argue whether the love of children on the part of parents is a natural thing which one may fully assume to exist. Certainly evidence beyond the need for collecting it indicates that parents, human and subhuman, do provide care for needy offspring. But there is also the opposite wish to abuse and to destroy children whom one may be responsible for. It is now axiomatic that one may be possessed of wishes of which one is not consciously aware and that manifest psychological disturbances may arise from such unconscious wishes. If indeed there is even a relatively ubiquitous unconscious wish to abuse and destroy children, it would certainly be therapeutic to make it conscious.

In a paper called "A Child Is Being Beaten" Sigmund Freud observed that the fantasy of a child being beaten was present in a surprisingly large proportion of his patients. He indicated that patients confess to the fantasy only with hesitation, that the subject is met with great resistance in analysis, and that even more shame and guilt are associated with this fantasy than with sexual wishes.[14]

Investigators directly concerned with child abuse suggest that such a wish may be widespread:

Many adults who never abuse children in real life may harbor abusive fantasies and impulses toward them at one time or another, yet be able to control these impulses and fantasies.[15]

All of us are certainly capable of cruelty; rare indeed is the man who has never felt the urge to strike out at a screaming child. Most of us are able to suppress this desire for violence

[14] S. Freud, *Collected Papers,* Vol. 2, J. Riviere (Trans.) (London: Hogarth, 1950), p. 172.

[15] D. G. Gil, "A Nationwide Epidemiologic Study of Child Abuse—Progress Report." Presented at the National Conference on Social Welfare, Chicago, June 1966.

and are filled with shame for harboring such brutal thoughts.[16]

Fleeting death wishes against the children must occur in most parents—which of them has not at some time thought, or even said, "Oh, drat the child"?—but these wishes often remain unconscious since there is a strong prejudice against their recognition.[17]

The parent's wish to commit infanticide . . . may be more prevalent than any of us would like to think. . . . Among the patients whom I have treated, there is no lack of evidence that such a wish exists.[18]

This last writer continues with some examples:

A mother who brought her twelve-year-old son for treatment had been helped over the acute phase of a postpartum psychosis and described her overpowering wish to kill him and herself during his first two years of life. Although she felt that she had recovered from this feeling, her communications established an intensely destructive attitude toward him. In another case of an adolescent boy who tried to commit suicide, the mother revealed that her first impulse after his birth was to "shove him back up." The mother of a four-and-a-half-year-old girl informed me in her third interview that she was constantly preoccupied with wanting to kill her daughter. She described an incident at swimming after which she reported that the little girl had stated, "Mommy

[16] F. M. Nomura, "The Battered Child 'Syndrome,'" *Hawaii Medical Journal,* 1966, *25,* 388.

[17] E. S. Stern, "The Medea Complex: The Mother's Homicidal Wishes to Her Child," *Journal of Mental Science (British Journal of Psychiatry),* 1948, *94,* 329.

[18] D. Bloch, "Feelings That Kill: The Effect of the Wish for Infanticide in Neurotic Depression," *Psychoanalytic Review,* 1965, *52,* 51.

*really loves me; she didn't try to drown me; it was an acci-
dent." During the first session, when the child expressed a
wish to look down at the street from my roof-terrace, before
I could indicate a low board on which she could stand comfortably, her mother seized and swung her above the parapet
wall, holding her so that there was nothing between her and
the street but space. The child gasped and grew pale.*[19]

Gregory Zilboorg identified problems evoked by having to care for children as a major factor in a study of thirty
men and thirty-seven women in whom depressive reactions
occurred. He noted that the depressive reaction in the parent was associated with intense hostile feelings, characteristically unconscious, toward the children. In discussing one
case, Zilboorg mused: "This again brings us close to the
puzzling problem of why parents hate their children."[20] The
way in which Zilboorg asked the question is most interesting.
He did not ask why *some* parents may hate their children.
But rather, his investigation of this large group of parents
led him to the more general form of the question.

This "puzzling problem" needs to be traced. I have
suggested the general hypothesis that child abuse is related
to population-resource balance. On the immediate level of
the relationship between parent and child, the critical
factor is that children may constitute a burden and a
threat, and thus they elicit the impulse to remove them
from being. Yet human society is contingent upon each
generation's accepting the burden of the next. Certainly, the
very existence of mankind on the face of the earth at the
present time attests to the fact that over and above any
tendencies to kill children are tendencies to undertake their
care, no matter how great the burden may be.

[19] Bloch, pp. 51–52.
[20] G. Zilboorg, "Depressive Reactions Related to Parenthood,"
American Journal of Psychiatry, 1931, *10,* 937.

Consider now the second aspect of identification, with the child-victim.[21] In some sense the child's feeling may be imagined to be that of confronting forces that would destroy him and of a tenuous impulse to do something desperate to save himself, to call for help against an attacker when that attacker is the sole source of help. Some children are abused in secret by those on whom they are dependent. They barely understand but are in fear. They keep the secret for fear that they will be savaged further for even revealing it. They learn to guard that secret well, so well that it is lost even to memory.

Thus, the very dynamics by which personalities are sometimes formed make it difficult to entertain the notion that parents have hostile impulses toward children. Sandor Rado characterized the infantile ego as engaging in a line of thought relevant to our topic:

"My parents must never punish me any more, they must only love me. Their image within my mind—my superego—will see to it that they need never again be angry with me. Of course my superego also must love me. But the function of my superego is to secure for me my parents' love; then it must be able to compel me to desist from certain actions. If necessary, it must be very severe with me, and, nevertheless, I shall love it." According to this description the formation of the superego is an attempt of the ego to realize its desire to transform the alternately "good" and "bad" parents into parents who are "only good." . . . Moreover, it must make up its mind to accord to the internalized parents (the superego) the right to be angry and severe on occasion; neverthe-

[21] The phenomenon of parents abusing their children is the ultimate of the "sickness unto death." See Soren Kierkegaard's *The Sickness unto Death*. Kierkegaard dealt quite directly with the fundamental story of child-killing, the Abraham-Isaac story, in his *Fear and Trembling*. These two books are quite properly issued in one volume: W. Lowrie (Trans.) (Princeton, N.J.: Princeton University Press, 1954).

16

less, the ego will not cease to love them and to desire their love.[22]

Justifying the superego puts one, as it were, on the side of the superego and presumably thus spares one from its anger. If one experiences some strength from the fact that one is an adult who is beholding the abuser, the impulse is to lash out against the abuser, repeating his psychodynamic pattern, except with the abuser as the victim. The irony of this reaction often escapes us. One is strongly drawn to this reaction to dissociate oneself from the abuser. To be angry at the abuser makes one feel that one cannot be an abuser, even though the reaction to the abuser is not essentially different from that of the abuser with respect to the child.

Another psychodynamic possibility is based on the simple fact that in the process of growing up the infantile self within each person must be overcome. If one conceives of growth as a movement from one age-associated role to other age-associated roles, then where do younger (and therefore older) roles go? Each of us carries within himself a dead baby, as it were, the baby each of us was and is no longer. The image of a parent abusing a child must, in some way, be evocative of the traces of the crisis we each experienced as we grew up—the crisis of having to outgrow our babyish dependency.

The emotional problem associated with thinking about child abuse is complicated by the fact that virtually all of us have been involved in corporal punishment of the young as the punished, the punishers, or both, even short of what we would generally think of as child abuse. The line between punishment in this sense and the kind of torment which I have been addressing may perhaps be quite thin psychologically. In the mind of the child the distinction be-

[22] S. Rado, "The Problem of Melancholia," *International Journal of Psychoanalysis*, 1928, 9, 433.

17

tween being hit-pained and being hit-injured is often too sophisticated to be appreciated. Indeed, it is always possible that the blow intended to cause only pain may injure. The child knows more of the infliction than of the restraint.

RESPONSIBILITY OF SOCIETY

It is tempting, as has been suggested, to subsume child abuse under psychopathology, to regard those who abuse children simply as insane. However, abusers in whom there is frank psychosis represent only a part of the total population of child abusers. It is even doubtful whether the proportion of the frankly psychotic among child abusers is much different from the proportion of the frankly psychotic in the noninstitutionalized population at large. In one investigation of eighty children who had been severly abused by their parents or parent substitutes, in only four cases, or 5 per cent, were the parents mentally ill in the conventional sense of the term.[23] This does not mean that in the other instances there is no evidence of conflict and even disturbance. Quite the contrary. But these other instances are not of such a nature that one can dismiss the people involved as being in a category different from the population at large.

Brandt F. Steele and Carl B. Pollock comment as follows on the relationship with other variables:

Basically . . . social, economic, and demographic factors . . . are somewhat irrelevant to the actual act of child beating. Unquestionably, social and economic difficulties and disasters put added stress in people's lives and contribute to behavior which might otherwise remain dormant. But such factors must be considered as incidental enhancers rather than necessary and sufficient causes. Not all parents who are unemployed and in financial straits, poor housing, shattered

[23] J. D. Delsordo, "Protective Casework for Abused Children," *Children,* 1963, *10,* 213–218.

marriages, and alcoholic difficulties abuse their children; nor does being an abstaining, devout Christian with a high I. Q., stable marriage, fine home, and plenty of money prevent attack on infants. These facts are well recognized by most of those who work in the area of child abuse. We have stressed them, however, because large segments of our culture, including many in the medical profession, are still prone to believe that child abuse occurs only among "bad people" of low socioecomic status. This is not true.[24]

The abuse of children entails two elements of existential crisis: (1) the existence of something which one regards as essential to life (2) in a situation which calls for its death that the remainder may live. Death itself is simple tragedy. Death, however, with imperative and choice becomes existential crisis. We must assume that as children are meaningful to and loved by parents who do not abuse them, so in some way must children also be loved by parents who do abuse them. In psychology we are accustomed to find opposites existing side by side. In most instances ambivalence tends to be resolved in the direction of the positive care and rearing of the children. In the instances which we have under consideration the resolution of the ambivalence has been reversed.

Two abiding certainties are connected with any social group, including nations. First, all members are mortal. Given the best of circumstances virtually everyone alive today will be dead within a hundred years. Second, the quality of human beings in a generation depends upon the kind of care which the earlier adult generation gives it. The certainty of man's mortality has been known for a long time. But the second certainty is hardly one which the world is sufficiently aware of. William Wordsworth indicated that "The child is father of the man." However, only in relatively

[24] Steele and Pollock, p. 108.

19

modern times has the full meaning of this phrase begun to be adequately appreciated.

Child abuse is a problem central to the larger question of how a generation of adults cares for its children. A group which does not spare resources for the raising of children and teaches those children to care for their children in turn guarantees its future for itself. If we understand the meanings of child abuse, we come to understand the general problem of the relationship among the generations. Child abuse is certainly an extreme form of this relationship, but it is methodologically sound to examine phenomena in their extreme instances. If we can come to understand how parents can abuse their own children, we may learn how a group may survive in an integral fashion beyond the limited existence of its individual members.

There has been some tendency in the last half century, a tendency which unfortunately has often faltered, for the society at large to assume greater responsibility for the care and protection of children whose parents have been unable or unwilling to do so. One example of this tendency was the formation of the juvenile court,[25] which was initially established in Chicago at the turn of the century. Central to the ideology of the juvenile court is the concept of *parens patriae,* the idea that the state has the ultimate responsibility of parenthood. Another important example is that already mentioned, the passage of legislation making the reporting of child abuse mandatory.[26] Whatever the practical consequences of such legislation, the very fact that there could be enough discussion and will to make such laws suggests perhaps that the taboo has been weakened and that the responsibility of the society at large has increased with respect to this problem.

[25] See N. K. Teeters and J. O. Reinemann, *The Challenge of Delinquency* (Englewood Cliffs, N.J.: Prentic-Hall, 1950).

[26] See M. G. Paulsen, "The Law and Abused Children," in Helfer and Kempe, pp. 175–200.

The right of parents to kill their children has, over the centuries, been considerably modified. The right to life was certainly not taken for granted in Rome or in other earlier cultures. Immanuel Kant dealt with this right as follows:

From the fact of procreation in the union thus constituted, there follows the duty of preserving and rearing children as the products of this union. Accordingly children, as persons, have, at the same time, an original congenital right —distinguished from mere hereditary right—to be reared by the care of their parents till they are capable of maintaining themselves; and this provision becomes immediately theirs by law, without any particular juridical act being required to determine it.

For what is thus produced is a person, and it is impossible to think of a being endowed with personal freedom as produced merely by a physical process. And hence, in the practical relation, it is quite a correct and even a necessary idea to regard the act of generation as a process by which a person is brought without his consent into the world, and placed in it by the responsible free will of others. This act, therefore, attaches an obligation to the parents to make their children—as far as their power goes—contented with the condition thus acquired. Hence parents cannot regard their child, as, in a manner, a thing of their own making, for a being endowed with freedom cannot be so regarded. Nor, consequently, have they a right to destroy it as if it were their own property, or even to leave it to chance, because they have brought a being into the world who becomes in fact a citizen of the world, and they have placed that being in a state which they cannot be left to treat with indifference, even according to the natural conceptions of right. . . .

From the duty thus indicated, there further necessarily arises the right of the parents to the management and training of the child, so long as it is itself incapable of

21

making proper use of its body as an organism, and of its mind as an understanding. This involves its nourishment and the care of its education. This includes, in general, the function of forming and developing it practically, that it may be able in the future to maintain and advance itself, and also its moral culture and development, the guilt of neglecting it falling upon the parents. All this training is to be continued till the child reaches the period of emancipation (emancipatio), as the age of practicable self-support. The parents then virtually renounce the parental right to command, as well as all claim to repayment for their previous care and trouble; for which care and trouble, after the process of education is complete, they can only appeal to the children by way of any claim, on the ground of the obligation of gratitude as a duty of virtue.

From the fact of personality in the children, it further follows that they can never be regarded as the property of the parents, but only as belonging to them by way of being in their possession, like other things that are held apart from the possession of all others and that can be brought back even against the will of the subjects.[27]

Running counter to the general sentiment expressed by Kant is the doctrine of parental immunity, which has existed in various forms throughout history. Parents have been held immune in suits involving cruel and inhumane treatment. They have even been held immune for falsely having a child placed in an insane asylum. A fifteen-year-old girl who had been raped by her father (who had in fact been convicted of the crime) was denied any recovery. The law hesitates to move against parents because such action may encourage wayward and disrespectful attitudes in children. Allowing a child to sue his parents could lead to friction in the home, and such friction could interfere with the right

[27] I. Kant, *The Philosophy of Law,* W. Hastie (Trans.) (Edinburgh: T. T. Clark, 1887), pp. 114–117.

of the parent to discipline a child.[28] On the other hand, "a common reaction, . . . when confronted with the brutal facts, is shock and anger. A natural consequence is a desire to exact retribution—to punish unnatural parents for their acts of cruelty." This retribution is sometimes unfortunate since, if the court fails to find the parents guilty, as it may because of the doctrine of immunity or for other reasons, it can be interpreted as a "license to continue to abuse."[29]

By implication, legislation making the reporting of child abuse mandatory indicates that the protection of children is not the restricted province of parents but rather the larger responsibility of the society as a whole, which is to take over when the parents fail either by willful injury or by neglect. There has, however, unfortunately been a gross lack in follow-up of such legislation. Virtually no money has been provided for servicing the new cases that have come to light. In discussing this situation, a reviewer of the legal situation in connection with child abuse sought to find out what was being spent. He cites a typical reply: "My understanding is that the juvenile courts and the Department of Welfare are absorbing any costs that may be involved." He indicates that exceptions in his survey were Massachusetts, which appropriated $100,000, and Illinois, which expended $50,000, which was to cover printing, publication, an emergency twenty-four hour phone service, and additional staff.[30]

An important ruling in connection with child abuse was handed down by Harold A. Felix of the Family Court of the State of New York in 1965. The ordinary rules of evidence are often too stringent to establish the facts of child

[28] K. D. McCloskey, "Case Notes. California Cases. Torts: Parental Liability to a Minor Child for Injuries Caused by Excessive Punishment," *Hastings Law Journal*, 1960, *11*, 335–337.
[29] V. De Francis, *Child Abuse Legislation: Analysis and Study of Mandatory Reporting Laws in the United States* (Denver: American Humane Association, 1966), p. 3.
[30] Paulsen, p. 199.

abuse. Child abuse, carried on out of sight of anyone but the abuser, with the child too immature to be a witness on his own behalf, requires some new principle of evidence. In such cases circumstantial evidence is admissible: "The principle of *res ipsa loquitur* [the thing speaks for itself] is applicable, . . . the infant showing signs of having been beaten since proof of abuse by parents which occurs in the privacy of the home is difficult. Accordingly, the condition of the child speaks for itself, thus permitting an inference of neglect to be drawn from proof of the child's age and condition."[31] Although this ruling and similar ones are openings for assumption of responsibility for abused children by the society as a whole, little rectification of the situation can take place until the resources of society are generously provided for this purpose.

A reasonable solution to the problem of child abuse can come about only if there is a large-scale acceptance that the welfare of children is of concern to the whole of the society and that the welfare and very survival of the total society critically depend upon the welfare of its children. I am not suggesting centralization of authority. Rather, what is needed is the enlargement of material and social supports for parents and an increased sensitivity to fundamental rights for all. To put it most simply, the solution to the problem of child abuse is a working democracy in which basic human rights, including security of person, are guaranteed for all, including children.

[31] I am indebted to Judge Felix for providing me with a copy of his judgment.

TWO

Annals of
the Damned

A discrepancy exists between the magnitude and significance of child abuse in history and its documentation. Certainly one must hesitate in making assertions about the nonexistence of what is not found, for no search is ever so very thorough as to preclude the possibility of gross oversight. Nonetheless, in the material that generally comes to the attention of educated persons of the contemporary world, child abuse and infanticide are not among the most prominent topics. Yet I am of the opinion that this phenomenon is of substantially greater significance for understanding the total condition of mankind than has been commonly recognized. It is certainly beyond the simple professional interests of physicians, social workers, psychologists, and the like. In this chapter I draw attention to a few of the items in the literature which at least hint at the possible magnitude and significance of the problem.

To set the stage with some familiar examples, Shakespeare was profoundly aware of the way in which the infanticidal impulse in a mother could be triggered. He has Lady Macbeth say:

> *I have given suck, and know*
> *How tender 'tis to love the babe that milks me;*
> *I would while it was smiling in my face*
> *Have pluck'd my nipple from his boneless gums,*
> *And dash'd the brains out, had I so sworn as you*
> *Have done to this.*[1]

In *King John* he gives us the following example:

Salisbury : His passion is so ripe it needs must break.
Pembroke: And when it breaks, I fear will issue thence
The foul corruption of a sweet child's death.[2]

UBIQUITY OF INFANTICIDE

The interpretation of the Bible as a historical record may be debated by scholars. But the Bible can certainly be read as a record of what has concerned man without the benefit of detailed historic scholarship. Allusions to infanticide in the Bible are numerous, suggesting both the existence of a horrible reality as well as an effort on the part of the authors of the Bible and sponsors of the biblical message to counteract it. Christianity began with a holocaust of the Slaughter of the Innocents (which I have borrowed[3] to en-

---

[1] *Macbeth,* act 1, sc. 7, lines 54–59.
[2] Act 4, sc. 2, lines 79–81.
[3] L. Adelson, "Slaughter of the Innocents," *New England Journal of Medicine,* 1961, *264,* 1345–1349.

title this volume), from which Jesus is presumed to have saved. According to Matthew's account of Jesus' birth, "Then Herod, when he saw that he was mocked of the wise men, was exceeding wroth and sent forth and slew all the children that were in Bethlehem and in all the coasts thereof, from two years old and under, according to the time which he had diligently inquired of the wise men."[4] In commemoration of these events, Innocents Day was celebrated historically in most Christian countries by ritually whipping children.[5]

The narrative of Jesus being saved from a holocaust of infant slaughter parallels a similar story in the Old Testament about Moses. Pharaoh is depicted as ordering the slaying of the children, first by ordering the midwives to do it and then, upon his learning that they failed to carry out his orders, by ordering that the male children be cast in the river.[6] According to the biblical story, Moses' mother defers at least partially by putting the baby Moses in the river, in a box, from which he is rescued by an Egyptian princess, as the story has it.

Earlier in the biblical account we have the story of Abraham putting his son Isaac upon the altar to slay him.[7] A folk myth similar to the narratives of Jesus and Moses rounds out the biblical story in connection with Abraham:

Nimrod, the great king of Babylon, was a great astrologer himself, and in the stars, which he constantly consulted, he had read that a boy would be born in Mesopotamia who would one day declare war unto the king and his religion and in the end come forth victorious. Greatly troubled in his mind, Nimrod asked his councilors for advice. At the advice of the latter, he built a big house eighty yards in length and

---

[4] Matt. 2:16.
[5] R. E. Helfer and C. H. Kempe (Eds.), *The Battered Child* (Chicago: Chicago University Press, 1968), p. 3.
[6] Exod. 1:9ff.
[7] Gen. 22:1ff.

27

sixty in breadth, wherein all the women about to give birth to a child were kept and closely watched. The midwives and nurses were commanded to kill unhesitatingly every newborn boy but to bestow rich presents upon those women who would give birth to a girl. Thus seventy thousand boys were massacred by order of the King Nimrod. Thereupon the angels in heaven implored the Lord of the Universe, the God of Justice, to wreak vengeance upon Nimrod and to punish him for his massacre of the innocent babies. And the Lord of the Universe replied: "I slumber not, neither do I sleep; in good time the cruel murderer will be punished and his deeds avenged." Soon Emtelai, the wife of Terah, was about to give birth to a child and was brought into custody by order of the king. But lo! a miracle happened and all the outward signs of her pregnancy disappeared, so that she was set free. And when the day of her delivery approached, she secretly left the town and concealed herself in a cave. Here she bore a son, Abraham, the radiance of whose countenance shed a brilliant light in the dark cave. Wrapping the child in one of her garments, she left it there, relying upon the mercy of God Almighty. And when the Lord of the Universe heard the wailing of the boy, He sent His angel Gabriel into the cave to feed the baby. The angel Gabriel offered one finger of his right hand to the crying babe to suck, and lo! from the angelic finger milk flowed abundantly.[8]

The numerous other references to the killing of children in the Bible indicate, at the very least, that it concerned the writers who composed the biblical record. The prophets often preached against the killing of children and most surely were not addressing themselves idly to the issue.

There is evidence that hell was orginally the place where children were burned. The New Testament word for hell is Gehenna, a corruption of Ge-Hinnom. Hinnom is a

[8] A. S. Rappoport, *Myth and Legend of Ancient Israel,* Vol. 1 (New York: Ktav, 1966), pp. 228–229.

28

valley near Jerusalem which the prophets railed against as the place where the children were destroyed. Jeremiah called it the "valley of slaughter."[9] It was in such valleys that children were killed at least in the eras of Solomon, Ahaz, and Manasseh, in biblical history. Solomon "did evil in the sight of the Lord" and "did . . . build a high place for Chemosh . . . and for Molech,"[10] gods to whom living children were sacrified by burning. King Ahaz "burnt incense in the valley of the son of Hinnom and burnt his children in the fire."[11] King Manasseh "caused his children to pass through the fire in the valley of the son of Hinnom."[12] This valley took on sinister significance and played a role in the fashioning of virtually all myths of hell since then. It was later turned into a garbage dump that burned continuously, providing an image of the continuous burning of the fires of hell.

The immurement of children in the foundations of erected structures has an ancient history. Joshua's curse against anyone who would rebuild Jericho was "he shall lay the foundation thereof in his firstborn, and in his youngest son shall he set up the gates of it."[13] And this curse is fulfilled some time later, if we take the biblical account as historical. "In his days did Hiel the Bethelite build Jericho: he laid the foundation thereof in Abiram, his firstborn, and set up the gates thereof in his youngest son, Segub, according to the work of the Lord, which he spake by Joshua the son of Nun."[14] Archaeological finds have revealed many jars among the Canaanites with bones of newborn infants. The jars had been buried under house corners, thresholds, and floors.[15]

[9] Jer. 7:32.
[10] 1 Kings 11:7.
[11] 2 Chron. 28:3.
[12] 2 Chron. 33:6.
[13] Josh. 6:26.
[14] 1 Kings 16:34.
[15] C. F. Potter, "Infanticides," in M. Leach (Ed.), *Dictionary of Folklore, Mythology, and Legend,* Vol. 1 (New York: Funk and Wagnalls, 1949), pp. 522–524.

When a king died to whom he was grateful, a man buried his two daughters with him, in 587 B.C. in China. As late as 1873 female infanticide was permitted in China. "It was, and may still be, the custom for new pottery furnaces in the Kiang-si province to be consecrated with the secret shedding of children's blood."[16] There is reason to believe that children were immured in the dikes of Oldenburg until the seventeenth century.[17] The practice of putting children into foundations is evidently an ancient practice in India as well.[18] As late as 1843, when a new bridge was to be built in Halle, there was a widespread suspicion that a child was wanted to put into the foundation.[19]

Infanticide has been reported as a regular feature of numerous cultures including the Eskimo, Polynesian, Egyptian, Chinese, Scandinavian, African, American Indian, and Australian aborigine. In the Hawaiian Islands it was customary to kill all children after the third or fourth. Among the Australian aborigines if a woman had two children and was forced to march because of lack of food or water and if she could not carry two children, the younger one was customarily killed.[20] James Frazer indicated that the Polynesians regularly killed two-thirds of their offspring. During the first half of the nineteenth century Rev. J. M. Orsmond reported on this condition in Tahiti. (His manuscripts were published by his granddaughter in 1928 under the title *Ancient Tahiti.*) More than two-thirds of the children were destroyed "generally before seeing the light of day. Sometimes in drawing their first breath they were throttled to death, being called *tamari'i hia* (children throttled)." The

[16] E. S. Stern, "The Medea Complex: The Mother's Homicidal Wishes to Her Child," *The Journal of Mental Science* (*The British Journal of Psychiatry*), 1948, *94*, 324–325.

[17] Stern, p. 327.

[18] Stern, p. 352.

[19] E. B. Taylor, *Primitive Culture* (5th ed.), Vol. 1 (London: J. Murray, 1913), p. 104.

[20] W. G. Sumner, *Folkways* (Boston: Ginn, 1906), p. 315.

Orsmond manuscripts indicate a dramatic relationship between infanticide and social class, there being a dramatic difference in obligation to commit infanticide depending upon which social class the parents belonged to. The lowest members of the society, who had only small and few tattoos, were obliged to kill their children. "If any saved their babes, they were dismissed in disgrace from the society." However, members of higher classes, virtually covered by tattoos, were obligated to refrain from killing their children.[21] According to one estimate, six-sevenths of the population of India practiced female infanticide prior to the present century.[22] The British government in the early nineteenth century attempted to stop the custom of Hindu women in Bengal of casting children into the Ganges. The British also forced the people to substitute a sheep for the child that was customarily sacrificed on Friday evening at the shrine of Kali at the great Saiva Temple at Tanjore.

In classical times, Seneca, Plato, and Aristotle maintained that the killing of defective children was a wise custom. The twelve tablets of Romulus of ancient Rome indicate quite clearly that the exposure of newborn infants was a rather common occurrence. Roman law gave the father the power of life and death over his children. This law was invoked against children not only in infancy and childhood, but also in later life. Thus, Fulvius, a Roman senator, had his son put to death because the son had joined the Catilinarian conspiracy in 63–62 B.C. The Institutes of Justinian boasted, "The legal power which we have over our children is peculiar to Roman citizens, for no other men have the power over their children that we have."[23] William Lecky said that infanticide was "the crying vice of the [Roman]

---

[21] Cited in Potter, pp. 522–523.
[22] Sumner, p. 318.
[23] Cited in R. W. Lee, *The Elements of Roman Law* (London: Sweet and Maxwell, 1956), p. 80.

31

empire."[24] Later on, Constantine abolished the law, but allowed the sale of newborn children into slavery.[25]

In numerous places in history the child was not considered to have a claim on life until certain ceremonies were performed—with baptism still remaining with us as an affirmation of the child's right to a life.

The Egyptian midwife had to pray for the soul to join the newborn infant, and the Babylonian father had to impart his spirit into the child by blowing into its face and then giving it his name or the name of one of his ancestors, thus bestowing upon it a soul. In this manner a child was assured of life. The Frisian father could destroy or otherwise dispose of his infant only before it had taken food—here, to give food was life-giving. In Athens the amphidroma ceremony was performed as a rule on the fifth day of life, when the new baby was carried by its nurse around the ancestral hearth to receive consecration and a name. If the child was not wanted, the father had to dispose of it before the amphidroma. In general, the longer a child was permitted to live, the more the parents became attached to him, and thus the longer he survived the greater his chances for social recognition and parental care.[26]

In early Scandinavia:

The father would expose a child to take revenge for an insult on the part of his wife. Or the child of a concubine might be killed because of the jealousy of the right wife. A brother habitually killed the child of his sister if its birth caused the death of the mother. The old Vikings extended a spear to the newborn boy. If the child seized it, it was

[24] Cited in Sumner, p. 319.
[25] Lee, p. 61.
[26] Helfer and Kempe, p. 6.

allowed to live. Because Olver, a powerful Viking, did not administer this test, he was nicknamed "barnakarl," children's man. More commonly the life of the child was made dependent upon the performance of a fixed ceremony similar to our modern ceremony of baptism. This ceremony is usually called "Wasserweihe."

Immediately after the birth of a child the father was summoned, and the child was placed either on his knee or on the floor before him. If he decided that the child should live he took it up in his arms. Then water was poured on the child, a name was given, and generally it was presented with a gift. Not until then was nourishment given to the child. If the child was not taken up by the father, it was immediately exposed or killed without baptism and without food. If either of these two conditions had been fulfilled, it became illegal to kill a child. Another important element was attached to this ceremony. From the time that a child was baptized, it had property rights. The importance attached to this fact is attested by the long survival of the custom of reckoning the attainment of property rights from time of baptism. In Sweden this custom remained until 1734, in Norway until 1854, and in Denmark until 1857.[27]

Ritualized murder of children was also not unknown. A relatively popular verse in England, which was part of a game called "Jack's Alive and Likely to Live," was:

Jack's alive and likely to live.
If he dies in your hand you've a forfeit to give.

Or

Jack's alive and in very good health,
If he dies in your hand you must look at yourself.

[27] O. H. Werner, *The Unmarried Mother in German Literature* (New York: Columbia University Press, 1917), pp. 20–21.

This game and its verses are believed to have been connected with a medieval heretical sect called Boni Homines. This group was accused by the orthodox and the clergy of engaging in a rite in which a deliberately injured child was passed around from hand to hand, with the idea that the spirit of the child would descend on the person in whose arms he died.[28]

Such considerations suggest that the repeated charge of ritual murder of children may be taken as indicative of the thought of infanticide. This accusation has been made against Jews throughout the history of Christianity.[29] Indeed, it has lasted through to modern times. In 1899 a Jewish man was so charged in Bohemia,[30] and two pamphleteers in 1935 in New York renewed the accusation that Jews are under obligation to kill for ritual purposes.[31]

The suspicion exists that the popular Scottish song of John Barleycorn, written down and adumbrated by Robert Burns, is based on a ritual in which a human representative of John Barleycorn was ground with the grain:[32]

> *There was three kings unto the east,*
> *Three kings both great and high,*

[28] A. H. Krappe, *The Science of Folklore* (London: Methuen, 1965), p. 197.

[29] J. Trachtenberg, *The Devil and the Jews: The Medieval Conception of the Jew and Its Relation to Modern Anti-Semitism* (New Haven, Conn.: Yale University Press, 1943), recounts this history in detail.

[30] M. Grunwald, *History of the Jews in Vienna* (Philadelphia: Jewish Publication Society of America, 1936), p. 429.

[31] *The Jewish Encyclopedia*, Vol. 2, p. 401.

[32] Krappe, p. 325. That the popular culture clearly associates the Christian story with infanticide and, strangely, attributes it to the three kings of the East is most interesting. The appearance of three men in connection with the birth or death of a child is an ancient theme repeated at least three times in the Bible: to announce the coming of Isaac, to comfort Job on the death of his children, and at the birth of Jesus. See also: "Though these three men were in it, as I live, saith the Lord God, they shall deliver neither sons nor daughters." Ezek. 14:18.

And they hae sworn a solemn oath
John Barleycorn should die.[33]

William Graham Sumner, one of the pioneers of modern sociology, was one of the very few modern social scientists to recognize the killing of children as a significant feature of human social history. He wrote: "Child sacrifice expresses the deepest horror and suffering produced by the experience of the human lot. Men must do it. Their interests demand it, however much it might pain them. Human sacrifice may be said to have been universal. . . . It lasted down to the half-civilized stage of all nations and has barely ceased amongst the present half-civilized peoples."[34]

The depth of the significance of infanticide in European thought is suggested by Goethe's use of the theme in *Faust*. Evidently no particular instance influenced Goethe. A scholar who sought to find a single background event for the infanticide episode in *Faust* concluded: "The fact is that infanticide was so common in the last half of the eighteenth century that unless a specific case is mentioned by the writer himself or by his immediate friends, no one case can be looked upon as the sole source of any particular literary production.[35] Goethe was indeed the author of a petition to Duke Karl August in which he discussed the case of an unmarried mother who had been excommunicated from the church and who was being required to undergo excruciating penance in order to become a member again.[36] But it is hardly likely that this or any other single instance was the

---

[33] R. Burns, *The Complete Poems of Robert Burns,* Vol. 2 (London: Waverley, 1927), p. 142. The ungrammatical *was* is Burns's doing. He did not claim originality for John Barleycorn, rather that he had heard the old song and could remember only the first three verses and "some scraps" which he had "interwoven here and there in the piece." It is evidently of ancient origin.

[34] Sumner, p. 553.
[35] Werner, p. 8.
[36] Werner, p. 28.

model for Gretchen, who was impregnated by Faust and who killed her child in Goethe's great drama.

In 1781 a contest was held in German-speaking Europe for the best essay on how to prevent infanticide. Four hundred essays were submitted, provoking one commentator at the time to say, "The prize question, how infanticide might be checked, has alarmed so many scholars in all the faculties that one is amazed at the large number of essays submitted."[37] Johann Heinrich Pestalozzi, the distinguished educator, was stimulated by the contest to write an essay on the topic, although he did not submit it but published it elsewhere. He specifically discussed fifteen cases in one chapter from the records in the archives at Neuhof.

Infanticide! Do I dream or am I awake! Is it possible, this deed? Does it happen? Does the unnamed happen? No, not the unnamed, the named, the crime which has found expression in words. Conceal thy face, O Century! Bow down, O Europe! From the seats of justice comes the answer: my children are killed by the thousands at the hands of those who give birth to them. . . . In vain runs the blood of thy infanticides, O Europe! Let thy rulers remove the causes of their despair, and thou wilt save their children. Thy sword has killed many an infanticide during my time, but I shall tell the story of the first one only![38]

The executions by decapitation for infanticide in the eighteenth century were, as stated by one of the contributors to the contest, "without number."[39] Pestalozzi cited a letter from a minister saying, "I am discovering daily from examples which occur in my own congregation the horrifying extent of infanticide."[40]

[37] Cited in Werner, p. 4.
[38] Cited in Werner, p. 7.
[39] Cited in Werner, p. 7.
[40] Cited in Werner, p. 8.

Frederick the Great, king of Prussia from 1740 to 1786, concerned himself particularly with the problems of infanticide. He abolished execution by sacking—in which the victim is put into a sack with rocks and thrown into a river—as a punishment for infanticide in the year of his coronation, substituting decapitation as more humane. He abolished church penance for unmarried mothers because as he put it, the punishment and the disgrace "give occasion to infanticide." He discussed punishment for infanticide in his *Dissertation sur les raisons d'etablir ou d'abroger les lois:*

Heaven knows that I do not for a moment excuse this horrible act of these Medeas, who, cruel to themselves and to the voice of blood, kill the future race. But I would that the reader might weigh all the prejudices of custom and deign to give some attention to the reflections that I am going to present. The laws, do they not attach infamy to clandestine childbirth? A girl only too easily fooled by the promise of a seducer, does she not find herself compelled by the very force of circumstances to choose between the loss of her honor and the elimination of the unhappy fruit that she has conceived? Is it not the fault of the laws to place a girl in such a desperate position? And does not the severity of the judges deprive the state of two subjects, the child which it forces the mother to kill and then the mother herself in expiation of her crime, a mother who may have intended to make it possible to repair her loss by becoming a legal mother and then to propagate legally? I know that they save an innumerable number of bastards to society, but would it not be better to take the evil by the roots and save all of these poor creatures who perish miserably, by abolishing the detriments attached to the results of an imprudent and secret love?[41]

In the seventeenth century Benedict Carpzov is

[41] Cited in Werner, pp. 35–36.

credited with having executed twenty thousand women for witchcraft, a large number having committed infanticide. His manner of execution was the prevalent one of sacking, to which he added the exquisite touch of joining live animals to the victim's fate and forcing her to sew the bag.[42] Burning, burying alive, and empaling were also common methods for execution of persons who engaged in infanticide.[43]

In England, the relationship between illegitimacy and infanticide was the topic of the very popular ballad of "The Cruel Mother":

1. *There was a lady came from York*
   All alone, alone and aloney,
   She fell in love with her father's clerk
   Down by the greenwood siding.

2. *When nine months was gone and past*
   Then she had two pretty babes born.

3. *She leaned herself against a thorn*
   There she had two pretty babes born.

4. *Then she cut her topknot from her head*
   And tied those babies' hands and legs.

5. *She took her penknife keen and sharp*
   And pierced those babies' tender hearts.

6. *She buried them under a marble stone*
   And then she said she would go home.

7. *As she was (going through) (a-going in) her father's hall*
   She spied those babes a-playing at a ball.

8. *"Oh babes, oh babes if (you were) (thou wast) mine*
   I would dress you up in silks so fine."

[42] Werner, p. 26.
[43] Werner, p. 26.

9. *"Oh mother dear when we were thine*
   You did not dress us up in silks so fine,

10. *"You took your topknot from your head*
   And tied us babies' hands and legs.

11. *"Then you took your penknife (long) (keen)*
   and sharp
   And pierced us babies' tender hearts.

12. *"It's seven years to roll a stone*
   And seven years to toll a bell.

13. *"It's mother dear oh we can't tell*
   Whether your portion is heaven or hell."[44]

Jonathan Swift's "A Modest Proposal" is an ironic clue to the underlying acute situation with respect to children in the eighteenth century in Britain.[45] Swift suggested that "whoever could find out a fair, cheap, and easy method for making these children sound and useful members of the Commonwealth would deserve so well of the public as to have his statue set up for a preserver of the nation."[46] It costs about two shillings to rear an infant for the first year, he said, and "no gentleman would repine to give ten shillings for the carcass of a good fat child, which . . . will make four dishes of nutritive meat, when he hath only some particular friend or his own family to dine with him." Thus, "the mother will have eight shillings neat profit and be fit for work till she produces another child."[47] He urges "the

---

[44] Cited in B. H. Bronson, *The Traditional Tunes of the Child Ballads*, Vol. 1 (Princeton, N.J.: Princeton University Press, 1959), p. 292.

[45] J. Swift, "A Modest Proposal for Preventing the Children of Ireland from Being a Burden to Their Parents or Country," in W. A. Eddy (Ed.), *Satires and Personal Writings* (London: Oxford University Press, 1965), pp. 21–31. Originally published in 1729.

[46] Swift, p. 21.

[47] Swift, pp. 24–25.

mother to let them suck plentifully in the last month, so as to render them plump and fat for a good table." One of the advantages of his scheme is that it would prevent "that horrid practice of women murdering their bastard children, alas! too frequent among us, sacrificing the poor innocent babes . . . more to avoid the expense than the shame."

About seventy years after Swift's "modest proposal" Thomas R. Malthus, in 1798, published the first version of his theory of population, reacting quite specifically to the vision of the "poverty and misery arising from a too rapid increase of population."[48] One of the remarkable aspects of Malthus' work is that although the greatest portion of his attention is devoted to the elaboration of what he called "the checks to population" to keep the balance of population to food supply, he was unable to adequately confront infanticide as a population check. This fact was pointed out by Darwin, who was cognizant of infanticide as a harsh, but fairly ubiquitous, reality.

[Malthus] has discussed these several checks, but he does not lay stress enough on what is probably the most important of all, namely infanticide . . . and the habit of procuring abortion. These practices now prevail in many quarters of the world; and infanticide seems formerly to have prevailed . . . on a still more extensive scale. These practices appear to have originated in savages recognizing the difficulty, or rather the impossibility, of supporting all the infants that are born.[49]

In spite of the mixed reaction to Malthus, the problem to which he addressed himself and which was the provocation of his essay still persisted critically almost a hun-

---

[48] T. R. Malthus, *An Essay on Population,* Vol. 1, M. P. Fogarty (Ed.) (London: J. M. Dent, 1958), p. 1.

[49] C. Darwin, *The Origin of Species* and *The Descent of Man* (New York: Modern Library, 1936), pp. 429–430.

dred years later, as witness the following "Song of the "Slums" popular in London in the late nineteenth century:

Up and down Pie Street,
The windows made of glass,
Call at number thirty-three,
You'll see a pretty lass.

Her name is Annie Robinson,
Catch her if you can,
She married Charlie Anderson,
Before he was a man.

Bread and dripping all the week,
Pig's head on Sunday,
Half a crown on Saturday night,
A farthing left for Monday.

She only bought a bonnet box,
He only bought a ladle,
So when the little baby came
It hadn't got no cradle.[50]

And it certainly persists today in most of the world.

The writings of Charles Dickens about the hard lot of children in the growing industrial society are indicative of the conditions in which he lived. "The Dickens" remains as a euphemism in our language for the beating of children. The beating scene depicted in his *David Copperfield* is only a pale literary reflection of the abuse of children that arose as their existence became increasingly a threat and a burden:

He walked me up to my room slowly and gravely—I am certain he had a delight in that formal parade of executing

[50] Quoted by D. Tennant, "The London Ragamuffin," *English Illustrated Magazine,* June 1885; cited by G. F. Northall, *English Folk-Rhymes* (London: Kegan Paul, Trench, Trubner, 1892), p. 550.

justice—and, when we got there, suddenly twisted my head under his arm.

"Mr. Murdstone! Sir!" I cried to him. "Don't! Pray don't beat me! I have tried to learn, sir, but I can't learn while you and Miss Murdstone are by. I can't indeed!"

"Can't you, indeed, David?" he said. "We'll try that." He had my head as in a vice, but I twined round him somehow and stopped him for a moment, entreating him not to beat me. It was only for a moment that I stopped him, for he sent me heavily an instant afterwards, and in the same instant I caught the hand with which he held me in my mouth, between my teeth, and bit it through. It sets my teeth on edge to think of it.

He beat me then, as if he would have beaten me to death. Above all the noise we made, I heard them running up the stairs and crying out—I heard my mother crying out— and Peggotty. Then he was gone; and the door was locked outside; and I was lying, fevered and hot and torn and sore and raging in my puny way, upon the floor.[51]

Some public awareness of the existence of the problem of child abuse accompanied the growth of the large urban-industrial centers of the late nineteenth and early twentieth centuries. The situation with respect to infanticide in Europe is manifested in the following summary from an 1890 edition of the *Encyclopaedia Britannica:*

The modern crime of infanticide shows no symptom of diminution in the leading nations of Europe. In all of them it is closely connected with illegitimacy in the class of farm and domestic servants. The crime is generally committed by the mother for the purpose of completing the concealment of her shame and, in other cases, where shame has not survived,

[51] C. Dickens, *David Copperfield*, Chapter IV, "I Fell into Disgrace."

in order to escape the burden of her child's support. The paramour sometimes aids in the crime, which is not confined to unmarried mothers.[52]

The deep unease associated with this problem is seen in this passage in the contradiction between the author's assignment of cause to "illegitimacy in the class of farm and domestic servants" and his statement that the crime "is not confined to unmarried mothers." The author describes the condition in the United Kingdom as follows:

It is difficult to say to what extent infanticide prevails in the United Kingdom. At one time a large number of children were murdered in England for the mere purpose of obtaining the burial money from a benefit club. In 1871 the House of Commons found it necessary to appoint a select committee "to inquire as to the best means of preventing the destruction of the lives of infants put out to hire by their parents." The trials of Margaret Waters and Mary Hall called attention to the infamous relations between the lying-in houses and the baby-farming houses of London. The form was gone through of paying a ridiculously insufficient sum for the maintenance of the child. "Improper and insufficient food," said the committee, "opiates, drugs, crowded rooms, bad air, want of cleanliness, and willful neglect are sure to be followed in a few months by diarrhea, convulsions, and wasting away." These unfortunate children were nearly all illegitimate, and the mere fact of their being hand nursed, and not breast, goes some way (according to the experience of the Foundling Hospital and the Magdalene Home) to explain the great mortality among them. Such children, when nursed by their mothers in the workhouse, generally live. The practical result of the committee of 1871 was the Act of 1872, . . . which provides for the compulsory registration of

[52] *Encyclopaedia Britannica* (9th ed., 1890), Vol. 13, p. 3.

all houses in which more than one child under the age of one year are received for a longer period than twenty-four hours. No license is granted by the justices of the peace unless the house is suitable for the purpose and its owner a person of good character and able to maintain the children. Offenses against the Act including willful neglect of the children even in a suitable house are punishable by a fine of £5 or six months' imprisonment with or without hard labor.[53]

Abortion is closely related to infanticide. In George Devereux's comprehensive cross-cultural investigation of abortion, he found evidence for abortion as a practice among 60 per cent of the groups studied. This statistic is itself interesting, but Devereux goes further in his analysis of the data. There are numerous indications, even where it is clear that abortion exists, that there is a taboo against talking about it. Devereux is brought to the opinion that *"abortion is an absolutely universal phenomenon and that it is impossible even to construct an imaginary social system in which no woman would ever at least feel impelled to abort."*[54] Given the likelihood that infanticide is functionally similar to abortion and is probably under an even greater taboo, one may entertain the possibility of a similar conclusion about the universality of at least an infanticidal impulse—if not a universal cross-cultural acting out of the infanticidal impulse.

MODERN PERIOD OF RECOGNITION

In very recent times public recognition of the problem of child abuse has grown substantially. The mass media have provided some excellent coverage, indicative of a growing ability on the part of the public to face the phenomenon.

[53] *Encyclopaedia Britannica* (9th ed., 1890), Vol. 13, p. 3.
[54] G. Devereux, *A Study of Abortion in Primitive Societies* (London: T. Yoseloff, 1960), p. 161; Devereux's italics.

Programs based on the theme have been developed in the *Ben Casey* and *Slattery's People* television series.[55] Hank Burchard published an excellent series in the *Washington Post,* which has been widely reprinted.

Stories of child abuse or stories which can be explained only on the hypothesis that a child has been willfully abused appear in the newspapers regularly. For example, the *Cleveland Plain Dealer* on February 4, 1965, indicated that a hearing had been set

to determine the cause of injuries suffered by an eight-month-old baby hospitalized for a month . . . with two broken arms, a broken left leg, a fingernail missing from his left hand and body scars. . . . The child's mother said he fell forward from an upholstered chair and that his arms apparently caught in the sides of the chair, policewomen reported.[56]

The following editorial, "The Abuse of Children," from the *New York Times* of June 27, 1969, is representative of the kind of sentiment which has been appearing frequently in the press:

The particular case investigated by the Judicial Relations Committee involved little Roxanne Felumero, the repeatedly abused three-year-old who was found dead in the East River not long ago, bruised and battered, the pockets of her clothes weighted with rocks. Her stepfather, accused of previously beating the little girl, has been charged with the vicious crime.

The findings by the committee that "if the Family Court and the complex of public and private agencies operating within it had functioned more effectively, Roxanne

---

[55] S. R. Zalba, "The Abused Child. I. A Summary of the Problem," *Social Work,* 1966, *4,* 3.

[56] Cited in Zalba, p. 3.

*Felumero would probably not have met her tragic death"
goes beyond this particular case to expose an incredible pattern of slipshod practices and procedures that have apparently become the norm. The committee's excellent report
points up institutional inefficiencies that endanger the health
and life of every child in the city needing society's protection.*

*This need is, unfortunately, a wide one. Nearly a
thousand child abuse cases were reported to the State Department of Social Services last year, a figure that officials
note is but the tip of a vast and ugly iceberg. It represents
a 30 per cent increase over the year before. In thirty-six of
the reported cases, children were killed. In others the injuries they received caused permanent damage. Viciously
brutal beatings by parents, stepparents, and guardians have
often left children permanently crippled, blind, and retarded.*

*The horrible abuse continues. Among the cases this
year, in addition to Roxanne Felumero, is that of an eigh-
teen-month-old baby in the Bronx who was hanged by her
wrists and savagely whipped with a belt, then cut down and
left to lie on the bathroom floor for almost two days suffering
from a broken arm. In Manhattan, a four-year-old died of
starvation and neglect. Etc., etc., etc.*

*The sheer horror of these situations, the utter help-
lessness and vulnerability of the children cry out for immediate action on the judicial committee's recommendations for changes that would both implement the state's new
child abuse law and go beyond it. One of the few good
things done at the last session of the legislature was enact-
ment of that law, which seeks to expedite child abuse cases
and guarantee children greater protection. It requires hospital admission personnel, social workers, and school officials,
along with doctors, to report suspected cases of child abuse.
It also requires exchange of information among the social
agencies involved.*

The judicial committee recommends a "central regis-

*try" of information covering court cases and relevant back-
ground data, including reports of child abuse and the results
of investigations which can help Family Court judges properly dispose of cases before them.*

*The committee's proposal that the rotation of judges
should be ended to permit a judge to follow a case to its conclusion could be carried out without delay. Other recommendations depend on additional funds from the city government. More warrant servers are needed. Legal representation should be extended those who petition the court in behalf of children. More court reporting officers are required
Despite budgetary difficulties, it is essential that the mayor
give sympathetic attention to these recommendations.*

*There is hardly a more heinous crime than the brutal
abuse of children by adults to whom they look for love and
protection. Society has been shamefully late in coming to
their protection—cruelty to animals was condemned in New
York before cruelty to children—and it has been unconscion-
ably lax in erecting adequate safeguards. The judicial committee in its soul-searching report indicts the courts and supporting agencies—and it indicts society as well.*[57]

Urbanization, industrialization, and technological
change, insofar as they changed the value of children and
parents to each other, informed the child abuse situation. In
the eighteenth century parents sometimes maimed their
children so they could be used to beg or be sold to circuses.[58]
The abolitionist movement in the United States, for which
Harriet Beecher Stowe's *Uncle Tom's Cabin* was so important a document, was at once a movement for the freeing
of slaves and for a humane orientation to the welfare of chil-

[57] © 1969 by The New York Times Company. Reprinted by permission.

[58] M. G. Morris and R. W. Gould, "Role Reversal: A Concept in
Dealing with Neglected/Battered Child Syndrome," in *The Neglected-Child
Syndrome* (New York: Child Welfare League of America, 1963).

dren. The abuses of children in earlier industrial settings evoked a reaction against it. "With the coming of the machine age, however, mere babies were subjected to terrible inhumanity by the factory systems. . . . Children from five years of age upward were worked sixteen hours at a time, sometimes with irons riveted around their ankles to keep them from running away. They were starved, beaten, and in many other ways maltreated. Many succumbed to occupational diseases, and some committed suicide; few survived for any length of time."[59] In the United States, the journalists of the early twentieth century devoted attention to the way in which children were being misused and abused in industrial settings. The whole question of child labor became a matter of considerable public attention and legislation. In the first decade of the twentieth century the muckrakers led the reforms of the period. John Spargo's *The Bitter Cry of the Children*[60] played a particularly significant role in bringing public attention to the problem and in the eventual passage of child labor legislation.

A clear recognition of the existence of child abuse may be dated in the United States from the Mary Ellen case in 1874. At that time no society for the prevention of cruelty to children existed. However, the American Society for the Prevention of Cruelty to Animals did. This society intervened in a case of extreme child abuse; and following this case the New York Society for the Prevention of Cruelty to Children came into being.[61] The growing consciousness of the existence of child abuse and neglect led to the formation in 1912 of the Children's Bureau, which the federal government set up to investigate and to report "upon all matters

[59] Helfer and Kempe, p. 11.

[60] J. Spargo, *The Bitter Cry of the Children* (New York: Grosset and Dunlap, 1909).

[61] V. J. Fontana, "The Neglect and Abuse of Children," *New York State Journal of Medicine*, 1964, *64*, 215.

pertaining to the welfare of children and child life among all classes of our people."[62]

For over three-quarters of a century, the medical literature has reported a strange bone anomaly in young children. Not until the use of the X-ray machine overcame the profound muteness of children with respect to abuses did interest develop in any socially self-conscious manner. The objectivity of the X-ray photograph helped to overcome the profound mental resistance to recognizing child abuse as a reality. At a meeting of the Medical Society of London on April 13, 1888, a sharp debate took place. S. West had read a paper on "acute periosteal swellings in several young infants of the same family, probably rickety in nature."

A child, aged five weeks, was brought by its mother, with the statement that its left arm had "dropped." A swelling . . . occupied the middle third of the shaft of the left humerus. . . . Similar swellings were found on the right humerus and on the left femur. There were some slight bruises on the ribs. . . . The patient was the fifth child. . . . The first swelling came on the ninth day, the second in the fourth week, and the last two days before it came under observation. Of the other children the eldest was similarly affected at the age of a week. . . . The second . . . was never so affected. The third and also the fourth . . . were both affected. . . . The second case was seen in a child of the brother of the father of the previous children. It was a girl infant aged three weeks and had developed a swelling of the left humerus a week before being seen. . . . This patient was the fourth child. The first . . . had been well always. The second . . . had had both arms and legs affected in the same way at the same age. . . . That these were cases of early rickets could not, however, be doubted,

[62] M. M. Eliot, "Fifty Years of Public Responsibility for Actions in Behalf of Children," *American Journal of Public Health,* 1962, 52, 576–591.

on account of the evidence of rickets in the family and of the absence of any other assignable cause.[63]

The considerable discussion reported in the proceedings by the physicians present indicated serious doubts that rickets could be the cause of this strange disease. The multiplicity of the lesions, the fact that "the stress of the disease fell on the middle of the shaft," and the fact that the symptoms appeared very early even among infants who were breast fed were cited to suggest that rickets diagnoses were most unlikely. Yet, no explicit mention is made in this paper of what today we must recognize as another explanation.

The beginning of the modern period of recognition came in the middle 1940s with the appearance of reports in the medical literature of a strange "new syndrome," as an early paper called it,[64] by John Caffey, a physician at the College of Physicians and Surgeons at Columbia University and the Babies Hospital in New York City, and his associates. In a paper published in 1946 he wrote:

During the spring of 1938 we studied an infant whose principal lesions were scattered swellings deep in the soft tissues and scattered cortical thickenings in several bones. After an extensive investigation . . . it was evident that this patient suffered from none of the recognized conditions in which cortical thickenings had been found previously, such as scurvy, rickets, syphilis, bacterial osteitis, neoplastic disease, or traumatic injury. The three findings common to all of our patients were: (1) tender swelling deep in the soft tissues; (2) cortical thickenings in the skeleton; and (3) onset during

[63] S. West, "Acute Periosteal Swelling in Several Young Infants of the Same Family, Probably Rickety in Nature," *British Medical Journal,* 1888, *1,* 856.

[64] J. Caffey and W. A. Silverman, "Infantile Cortical Hyperostoses; Preliminary Report on a New Syndrome," *American Journal of Roentgenology,* 1945, *54,* 1 .

the first three months of life. . . . Other manifestations which were present in some patients but lacking in others were fever, pleurisy, anemia, and increase in the sedimentation rate of the erythrocytes. The course of the active disease was characteristically uneven. . . . All patients recovered after variable periods of many weeks or months. The cortical hyperostoses were visible roentgenographically months after the fever had subsided and after the soft tissue swellings had disappeared. After prolonged investigation of four patients, the cause remained undetermined. . . . Traumatic injury was not observed in a single case either at home or in the hospital.[65]

In another paper published in the same year he dealt with cases in which head injuries were accompanied by fractures in the bones of the arms and the legs. "For many years," he wrote, "we have been puzzled by the roentgen disclosure of fresh, healing, and healed multiple fractures in the long bones of infants whose principal disease was chronic subdural hematoma."[66]

Examination of the children raised many questions. What is the nature of this strange disease? Why is there blood in the vomit and feces? Why are there bluish and black spots on the face and the arms? Why are there fresh fractures, some in the process of healing and some already healed? Why are some of the children pale and undernourished? Why do they get better in the hospital and worse after being discharged? In one case, for example, the infant was discharged after a month in the hospital.

Four days later the mother brought the baby back to the

[65] J. Caffey, "Infantile Cortical Hyperostoses," *Journal of Pediatrics,* 1946, *29,* 541–542.

[66] J. Caffey, "Multiple Fractures in the Long Bones of Infants Suffering from Chronic Subdural Hematoma," *American Journal of Roentgenology,* 1946, *56,* 163.

hospital because the right leg had suddenly become tender and swollen and bruises had appeared under the left eye and in other parts of the body. The mother denied that any injury had occurred during the four days since discharge from the hospital. . . . Roentgenograms of the extremities disclosed that the bones in the arms were normal, but five fractures were visible in the shafts of the bones adjacent to the knee joints. . . . The patient remained in the hospital twenty-five days. The swelling and tenderness gradually disappeared.[67]

Caffey considered possible explanations for the observed phenomena: that the children injured themselves during a convulsion; that skeletal disease so weakened the bones that they were unusually vulnerable to trauma; or that the children were suffering from scurvy. All of these he rejected. Then he pointed out that in general medical opinion the cause of subdural hematoma is injury and that "negative history of trauma in so many cases can probably be best explained by assuming that sometimes lay observers do not properly evaluate ordinary but causally significant accidents, especially falls on the head, and that other important traumatic episodes pass unnoticed or forgotten by the time delayed cranial symptoms appear." But, most importantly, he said, "recognized injuries may be denied by mothers and nurses because injury to an infant implies negligence on the part of its caretaker."[68] But "trivial unrecognizable trauma" could not have caused the complete fractures in the bones of the arms and the legs. Other signs of injury were in evidence:

In each case unexplained fresh fractures appeared shortly after the patient had arrived home after discharge from the hospital. In one of these cases the infant was clearly un-

[67] Caffey, "Multiple Fractures . . . ," p. 166.
[68] Caffey, "Multiple Fractures . . . ," p. 172.

52

wanted by both parents, and this raised the question of intentional ill-treatment of the infant. . . . [This he followed with the laconic comment:] The evidence was inadequate to prove or disprove this point.[69]

He thus solved the mystery of the observed association of subdural hematoma with fractures of the long bones: "Some of the fractures in the long bones were caused by the same traumatic forces which were presumably responsible for the subdural hematoma."[70]

Caffey's earlier writings are distinguished by the fact that most of the important things he had to say were between the lines rather than within them. His great care of utterance reduced the impact of something which is hard to hear anyway.

A few years later, Frederic N. Silverman published a paper more explicit than that by Caffey. He indicated that the cause of such injuries to the bones could hardly be anything else than a severe blow of some kind.

It is surprising that physical trauma, probably the most common bone "disease" of infancy, should have certain roentgen manifestations which perplex physicians when discovered accidentally. . . . It is not often appreciated that many individuals responsible for the care of infants and children . . . may permit trauma and be unaware of it, may recognize trauma but forget or be reluctant to admit it, or may deliberately injure the child and deny it.[71]

In 1956 Caffey was invited to give the Mackenzie Davidson Memorial Lecture at the Annual Congress of the British Institute of Radiology in London. In that lecture he

[69] Caffey, "Multiple Fractures . . . ," p. 172.
[70] Caffey, "Multiple Fractures . . . ," p. 173.
[71] F. N. Silverman, "The Roentgen Manifestations of Unrecognized Skeletal Trauma," *American Journal of Roentgenology*, 1953, *69*, 413.

spoke very openly of the role of early diagnosis in saving abused children from further injury:

The correct early diagnosis of injury may be the only means by which the abused youngsters can be removed from their traumatic environment and their wrongdoers punished. Correct early diagnosis of injury . . . may be life-saving to some of these otherwise helpless youngsters, or it may prevent permanent crippling injuries to others.[72]

In discussing how the truth is avoided by physicians, Caffey indicated that the radiologist had "to stand his ground . . . and urge his trauma-insensitive colleagues to go into the history of trauma more fully or, when necessary, make a searching investigation of it himself."[73] The latter advice was in sharp contrast to the prevailing idea of the obligation of physicians in such cases.

However, no matter how much sense of social responsibility is manifested in the writing, no address to such a limited audience or publication in so highly specialized a journal as *The British Journal of Radiology* is likely to have great social consequences. Finally in 1962 the first relatively public acknowledgment of the problem was made in a way that could be consequential. It was a paper by six physicians, virtually a committee, in the *Journal of the American Medical Association,* probably the most widely circulated medical journal in the world. The physicians, enjoying the positive attitude toward physicians generally existing in the community, presented the problem as a medical syndrome, a disease in its own right, possessed of a set of symptoms, yet named by its cause. They called this disease the battered child syndrome and described it as follows:

[72] J. Caffey, "Some Traumatic Lesions in Growing Bones Other Than Fractures and Disclocations: Clinical and Radiological Features," *The British Journal of Radiology,* 1957, *30,* 238.

[73] Caffey, "Some Traumatic Lesions . . . ," p. 227.

54

*The battered child syndrome, a clinical condition in young
children who have received serious physical abuse, is a frequent cause of permanent injury or death. The syndrome
should be considered in any child exhibiting evidence of
fracture of any bone, subdural hematoma, failure to thrive,
soft tissue swellings, or skin bruising, in any child who dies
suddenly, or where the degree and type of injury is at vari-
ance with the history given regarding the occurrence of the
trauma.*[74]

In that paper they reported a nationwide survey of seventy-
one hospitals and seventy-seven district attorneys which
identified 749 children who had been victims of abuse.
Seventy-eight of the children had died, and 114 had suffered
permanent brain damage.

CHILD ABUSE AND INFANTICIDE

The reader may be wondering at the failure thus far to
distinguish between child abuse and infanticide. Such a distinction would, I believe, tend to confound the discussion. It
may appear that as in disciplining a child one may aim to
cause pain but not to injure, so may one seek to injure but
not kill a child. Clearly, this is a logical non sequitur. The
reader's defenses with respect to the pain-injury distinction
should not be brought to bear equally as defenses for the
injury-infanticide distinction. The latter is hardly the same.

The information available strongly suggests that in
some way, and at some level of consciousness, the aim of
those who abuse a child is to kill the child; the reason for
abusing him or her is to be rid of him or her. Many pieces
of evidence point to this conclusion. The very largest category of victims is very young children, the frequency of vic-

[74] C. H. Kempe, F. N. Silverman, B. F. Steele, W. Droegemueller,
and H. K. Silver, "The Battered-Child Syndrome," *Journal of the American
Medical Association*, 1962, *181*, 105.

timization being closely related to the degree of care that the age of the child demands. Children who have been directly victimized by beatings are often also victimized by neglect. The infliction of injury often follows a quite regular, and even ritualistic, pattern, as though to inflict cumulative injuries on the child. In many instances the parents were not interested in having the child, as manifested in the proportion of victims conceived out of wedlock. Only a small percentage of abusers are psychotic in any conventional sense of the term. And a high proportion of abused children die.

Thus, the most parsimonious explanation of child abuse is that the parents are trying to kill the child. However, in our culture murder of children is a serious criminal offense. The method of cumulative trauma allows infanticide to take place with relative immunity from detection, prosecution, and conviction.

Terrible as the thought is to entertain, child abuse may be a regression to a characteristic which comes very close to being "natural" to the human condition.

Infanticide is, in the wider sense of the term, primitive. It would be obscuring reality to call this trait "instinctive." It is not common to all mankind. Yet it comes so near being inherent in the primeval parent-child relationship that one is tempted to say of it: "Here, if anywhere, is a bit of behavior natural to primitive man!"[75]

Here then is a point, for we are not primitive. It is incumbent upon us to apprehend the nature of man as he is that we may be in a position to make man different. The role of man is to improve his natural and primitive condition. This is what civilization is all about.

[75] H. Aptekar, *Anjea: Infanticide, Abortion, and Contraception in Savage Society* (New York: William Godwin, 1931), p. 157.

THREE

What is Revealed unto Babes

In this chapter I take a different tack toward increasing our understanding of the phenomena of child abuse and infanticide by drawing attention to the literature for children. If, indeed, the matter has had the ubiquity and significance that I have suggested, then we should find indications of it in expressive literature which has had widespread circulation, on the assumption that in his fantasy the human being reveals what is of greatest moment to him. Even as it exists in the guise of fantasy so is the burden of its reality taken away. The use of fantasy to get at psychological reality is hardly new. Freud developed the method; it was further expounded by Henry A. Murray[1] and more recently

[1] See H. A. Murray, *Explorations in Personality* (New York: Ox-

has had fine use in the hands of David McClelland.[2] I have elsewhere gone into the many reasons why one should avoid methodological snobbery; the interested reader can pursue the technical methodological considerations which need not get repeated in this presentation.[3]

The Bible suggests that insights hidden from the wise and the prudent are often "revealed . . . unto babes."[4] I have borrowed that expression for the title of this chapter. Certainly the matter of child abuse has been hidden from many of the wise and prudent. It took the X-ray machine which penetrated through the flesh to the fractures in the bones, to make at least some of the wise and prudent cognizant of the degree to which children are mutilated in the flesh. However, if the wise and prudent have been systematically blind to the truth about child abuse, that truth has certainly been "revealed unto babes" in the children's folklore.

Freud argued that everyone "possesses in his unconscious an instrument by which he can interpret the expressions of the unconscious of another,"[5] and this observation should certainly apply to children. Children are sensitive to aggression directed against them, whether that aggression be overt or covert, conscious or unconscious. Alfred Adler observed that many children are most in fear of being struck.[6] In some way, the child who is hated registers that possibility somewhere in the recesses of his mind. Yet his immaturity stands in the way of his apprehending it; and the wisdom of

---

ford, 1958). H. A. Murray, *Thematic Apperception Test* (Cambridge, Mass.: Harvard University Press, 1943).

[2] D. C. McClelland, *The Achieving Society* (New York: Van Nostrand Reinhold, 1961).

[3] See D. Bakan, *On Method: Toward a Reconstruction of Psychological Investigation* (San Francisco: Jossey-Bass, 1967).

[4] Matt. 11:25; Luke 10:21.

[5] S. Freud, *Collected Papers*, Vol. 2 (London: Hogarth, 1950), p. 125.

[6] A. Adler, *The Practice and Theory of Individual Psychology*, P. Radin (Trans.) (New York: Humanities Press, 1951), p. 341.

psychological inheritance provides him with innocence, which is at once also a protection.

A crack in the innocence of both adults and children exists in the poems and stories adults recite for the entertainment of children and which children tend to appreciate. I dwell here on the infanticidal content of some of the most popular children's folklore in Western culture. The deepest wishes and concerns of people find their way into fiction and myth, while that same fiction and myth provide them with entertainment. Hard thoughts, thoughts that would otherwise be too unpleasant to think, smuggle their way into these fanciful renditions. There they are held fast in a frame of unbelief. Rhymes and stories live in relatively conscious thought precisely because a rhyme is manifestly nonsensical, and a fairy story is fictional and clearly made up, about some remote Jack or giant, not about a real person or a real event. Seeming untruth is a license for the story to live in conscious imagination. Some things are simply too terrible to think about if one believes them. Thus one does not believe them in order to make it possible to think about them. Paradoxically, then, the very disguise in a wrap of untruth allows truth to be conveyed and revealed.

One of the factors that makes for the rather remarkable identity that children's poems, particularly nursery rhymes, and stories tend to maintain is the child's insistence that when it is told again it should be "just the same."[7] I suggest that this trait is at least partly explained as resistance to having the meaning become too explicit, for a deviation would give the repressed material an opportunity to display itself more nakedly. This explanation is only a particular application of the general hypothesis that there is resistance to having the meanings become explicit in all forms of "fundamentalism" in which literalism is maintained on

[7] See I. Opie and P. Opie (Eds.), *The Oxford Dictionary of Nursery Rhymes* (London: Oxford University Press, 1962), p. 8.

59

principle. Rigidity with respect to the form of the recital is closely related to another psychological characteristic of children, their relative lack of ability to make differentiations. Children do not readily differentiate; they are likely to call a horse "doggie" and to call all men "Daddy." This fluidity is at the opposite pole of the rigidity of the form of recital and perhaps reinforces rigidity as a defense against the free identifications associated with this fluidity. In attempting to understand the meanings involved, we must recognize that both the rigidity of form and the fluidity of identification exist.

It is not surprising then that poems and stories that persist over long periods of time may allude to and express the deepest concerns of mankind while at the same time bearing an adequate protective cover so that they are not overtly threatening. Thus, one of the most blatantly infanticidal poems is

literature

> *Hush-a-bye, baby, on the tree top,*
> *When the wind blows the cradle will rock;*
> *When the bough breaks the cradle will fall,*
> *Down will come baby, cradle, and all.*

John B. Watson, the founder of behaviorism, asserted that there were only two original stimuli for fear in the child. One of these is a loud sound, and the other is a loss of support,[8] both of which are implied by the lullaby. In a certain sense the lullaby takes advantage of the fact that the child does not understand the words. It has the effect of cursing a person in a language he does not understand. If the child could understand the words, it would be difficult to find anything more threatening to say to him. This poem is, in fact, "the best known lullaby both in England and America," and "is regularly crooned in hundreds of thousands of homes at

[8] J. B. Watson, *Psychology from the Standpoint of a Behaviorist* (Philadelphia: Lippincott, 1924).

60

nightfall."[9] The very context of tenderness is license to allow the ugly thought which the poem contains to find expression.

In fact, the traditional feature of these poems and stories is part of their cover. Critical to their persistence over time is that they are selected again and again for repetition. Children's folklore is subject to natural selection in the same way biological forms are. Those that resonate well to the psychological conditions of mankind survive. The others pass into oblivion. Andrew Lang was quite right in calling folklore "the science of survivals." Part of the cover is that "Hush-a-Bye, Baby" is only "received." The mother who sings it to her child can hardly be accused of having invented or composed it. Indeed, she, having heard it from her parents, receives it with the blessing of her own superego and feels quite virtuous in repeating it to her own child.

A similar allusion to falling is in Humpty Dumpty. The fragility of the child is reflected in the egg. Humpty Dumpty has been one of the most popular nursery figures. The poem "is to be measured in thousands of years, or rather . . . it is so great that it cannot be measured at all."[10]

> *Humpty Dumpty sat on a wall,*
> *Humpty Dumpty had a great fall.*
> *All the king's horses and all the king's men*
> *Couldn't put Humpty together again.*

A German version of the poem is equally fatalistic about the consequence of a fall:

> *Wirgele-Wargele, auf der Bank,*
> *Fällt es 'runter, ist es krank,*

[9] Opie and Opie, p. 61.
[10] H. Bett, *Nursery Rhymes and Tales: Their Origin and History* (2nd ed.) (London: Methuen, 1924), p. 7.

Ist kein Doktor im ganzen Land,
Der dem Wirgele-Wargele helfen kann."[11]

Paul Simon, of the team of Simon and Garfunkel, wrote lyrics which appear to be a modern version of the Humpty Dumpty poem. The popularity of "Save the Life of My Child" strongly suggests that the psychological undercurrent which has sustained the existence of the Humpty Dumpty poem over the centuries still persists:

"Good God! Don't jump!"
A boy sat on the ledge.
An old man who had fainted was revived.
And everyone agreed it would be a miracle indeed
If the boy survived.

"Save the life of my child!"
Cried the desperate mother.

"All the king's horses and all the king's men" gets an interesting form in this modern version:

The woman from the supermarket
Ran to call the cops.
"He must be high on something," someone said. . . .

A patrol car passing by
Halted to a stop.
Said officer MacDougal in dismay:
"The force can't do a decent job
'Cause the kids got no respect
For the law today (and blah blah blah)."[12]

[11] Cited in Opie and Opie, p. 216.
[12] P. Simon and A. Garfunkel, *Bookends,* Columbia Records, 1968.

What is Revealed unto Babes

A fairly widely circulated magazine, *Humpty Dumpty's Magazine for Little Children,* has attached to the old Humpty Dumpty poem a new verse, bespeaking a dramatically new optimism. I cannot help but muse on the possibility that the very same social atmosphere which has made possible the new modern awareness of the child abuse problem may also be involved in the creation of the mood that allows the addition of this rhyme, which regularly appears in every edition.

> *But an American doctor with patience and glue*
> *Put Humpty together—better than new;*
> *And now he is healthy and back on the scene,*
> *Busily editing this magazine!*

The following poem has an ancient history:

> *Ladybird, ladybird,*
> *Fly away home.*
> *Your house is on fire,*
> *And your children all gone.*

It is "undoubtedly a relic of something once possessed of an awful significance."[13] Historical associations of this poem indicate that it has had sacred associations, especially with the figure of Mary. We may interpret *Tom Thumb, The Three Little Pigs,* and even Little Bo-Peep's lost sheep as suggestive of the jeopardy experienced by children.

Henry Bett,[14] a folklorist, interprets the various versions of the song and the game of "London Bridge" as possibly based on the historical practice of immuring a child in the foundation of a bridge (a practice I have referred to earlier). A characteristic feature of the game is the imprison-

[13] Opie and Opie, p. 263.
[14] Bett, p. 37.

ment of a child. In a German version the song finishes with "All creep through, all creep through, *We'll seize the last!*" The English rhyme indicates that lime and iron bars are not enough for London Bridge. The unspoken suggestion that only the life of a child can sustain it:

London Bridge has fallen down, fallen down, fallen down,
London Bridge has fallen down, My fair Lady!
How shall we build it up again, up again, up again,
How shall we build it up again? My fair Lady!
Build it up with lime and stone . . .
Stone and lime would wash away . . .
Build it up with iron bars . . .
Iron bars would bend and break . . .
Get a watch to watch all night . . .
Suppose the watch should fall asleep? . . .
Get a dog to bark all night . . .
Suppose the dog should get a bone? . . .
Get a cock to crow all night . . .
Suppose the cock should fly away? . . .
What has this poor prisoner done? . . .
Off to prison she must go.
My fair Lady!

Bett comments: "The accompanying game is concerned throughout with the capture of a victim, and both the action and the rhyme are eloquent of the dark rite of which they are a relic."

Fairy tales are appropriate for children somewhat older. They enter into the mind of the child easily. They become incorporated into the psychological processes because they have in them elements which are eternal in the experience of the human child and eternal in the relations between children and their parents. In the minds of many children the reality and the fairy tale blend easily into one another, not only because the child cannot discriminate between reality and fairy tale but because reality and fairy tale are so close to each other. The fairy tale is a representation of the important problems of life, which can be thought about in a way which is not immediately threatening. It may represent the fulfillment of a wish. It may be a rehearsal of a method of coping with a problem. It may be a warning delivered by adults to children.

The term *fairy tale* means stories in which there are fairies or simply fanciful traditional stories for children in the common folklore. The theme of getting rid of children by abandonment or by killing them is present in most of them. In one careful, scholarly treatment of the fairy tale in the first sense, the author tells us that "the thing that everyone knows about the fairies is that they covet human children and steal them whenever they can. No account of fairies is complete without mention of this practice."[15]

In the *Pied Piper of Hamelin,* in which the rats are drowned and the children are taken away, the psychological identification of the drowning of the rats and the similar fate for the children is barely disguised.

Consider the story of *Hansel and Gretel.* It opens: "Hard by a great forest dwelt a poor woodcutter with his wife and his children." Here are some signals in the opening. Poverty often prevails in fairy tales, and gathering food is often depicted as a problem. Poverty is the beginning justification for the sacrifice of children. The story continues. The father says, "What is to become of us? How are we to feed our poor children, when we no longer have anything for ourselves?" The wicked stepmother, always it is the stepmother, for it is too hard to think this of a real mother, says, "I'll tell you what, husband. Early tomorrow morning we will take the children out into the forest to where it is the thickest. There we will light a fire for them and give each of them a piece of bread more. Then we will go to our

[15] K. M. Briggs, *The Fairies in English Tradition and Literature* (Chicago: University of Chicago Press, 1967), p. 115.

65

work and leave them alone. They will not find the way home, and we shall be rid of them." Or,

There was an old woman who lived in a shoe,
She had so many children she didn't know what to do.
She gave them some broth without any bread,
And whipped them all soundly, and sent them to bed.

In addition to these two examples of wicked women, we find the stepmother who abuses the child, as in *Cinderella*; the stepmother who is trying to poison her child, as in *Snow White* (whose only protection is the seven dwarfs, who are as other children); and always the wicked witch, who, in her house in the woods, is seeking to entice, kill, and eat children. In the Slavic folk literature, the ubiquitous Baba Yaga lived in the woods and put children in the oven and ate them.

The witch is, in fact, quite real in the history of the world. The kindly old woman who, often for a fee, received unwanted and often illegitimate children is an abiding figure. The fee paid to those whose business was to perform an appropriate "service of love" was at one time during the eighteenth century a half louis d'or[16] (around two dollars). The association of witchcraft with infanticide is indicated by the fact that the German term *hexe* did not apply originally to human beings at all, but to child-devouring demons.[17] For centuries, at least from the Volga to the Mississippi, from the Rhine to the Nile, the old witch has truly cackled, "Don't worry, Dearie. I will take good care of him!" And even perhaps added, "Oh, isn't he darling!" This is the reality behind the character of the witch of folklore. An interesting parenthetical point is the practice of punishing witches by dunking, as in Salem, Massachusetts. This was

[16] O. H. Werner, *The Unmarried Mother in German Literature* (New York: Columbia University Press, 1917), p. 7.
[17] *Encyclopaedia Britannica* (11th ed., 1911), Vol. 28, 755.

lex talionis, the law of retaliation, since one of the easiest and evidently most common ways of disposing of unwanted children was through drowning. As has been previously indicated, a characteristic punishment in Europe for women who killed their babies was sacking. The ducking stool was a relic of this earlier, more catastrophic form of punishing witches.

More recent counterparts of Baba Yaga and all her fairy-tale sisters in real life were persons who ran baby farms in industrial areas, receiving the babies from the female industrial workers as they went from lying-in places back to the factories; persons who, during the nineteenth century, collected insurance money on children who had the misfortune of dying at an early age; and those who broke the bones of children to elicit pity and then put them out to beg. The witch theme was renewed in Ira Levin's best-selling *Rosemary's Baby*[18] and in the very popular movie based on it. Here again we have the witches, with their main aim being to take away Rosemary's baby. The continuing psychological reality of the basic theme is clearly demonstrated by the great interest that the book and movie evoked in so many people.

When is the child to be given away? Under what conditions is the right of the child to exist in question? The *Rumpelstiltskin* (or *Tom Tit Tot*) story hints at the answer to this question. The mother of the child must surrender the baby to Rumpelstiltskin unless she can recall a certain proper name. Whose name is she to recall? I suggest that the story deals with the question of legitimacy. Only if the mother can readily call up the name of the father of the child may she keep the child. The historical practice of a woman's taking the name of her husband may be interpreted as a kind of mnemonic that she not forget his name, and it guarantees that the child has the name of the father. *Rose-*

---

[18] I. Levin, *Rosemary's Baby* (New York: Dell, 1968).

67

mary's Baby incorporates the *Rumpelstiltskin* story in the part where Rosemary struggles through the Scrabble letters to find the name of Levin's Rumpelstiltskin. She identifies the name by making *Steven Marcato* out of *Roman Castevet* as an anagram. Indeed, Levin, with Rosemary having identified her Rumpelstiltskin properly, allows her to keep the baby, consistent with the ancient tale.

The characteristic male counterpart for the infanticidal witch is the familiar giant. He is also variously bogeyman, sandman, ragman, gypsy, hunter, thief, kidnapper, magician. But infanticide or mutilation or exploitation of children is always present.

The Punch and Judy puppet show, a favorite entertainment of all peoples of Europe for centuries, had within it the murder by Mr. Punch of his child. In the Punch and Judy show we have the basic notion that children interfere with freedom of movement and freedom of sexual life. Goethe was influenced by this puppet show in the creation of his *Faust,* the nonresponsible, free-moving, sexually indulgent male. The Punch and Judy scripts were varied and were greatly improvised. But the infanticidal theme, and thus the barely disguised wish to kill the child that interfered with the free expression of Punch's sexuality, was characteristically a part of it. The following is from a ballad that dates in written form from the eighteenth century:

> *Oh! harken now to me awhile,*
> *A story I will tell you*
> *Of Mr. Punch, who was a vile*
> *Deceitful murderous fellow,*
> *Who had a wife, a child also,*
> *And both of matchless beauty;*
> *The infant's name I do not know,*
> *Its mother's name was Judy.*
> *Right tol do rol lol, etc.*

Judy finds out that "he kept a lady" and expresses her jealousy and anger.

> *Then Punch he in a passion flew,*
> *And took it so in dudgeon,*
> *He fairly split her head in two—*
> *Oh! monster!—with a bludgeon.*
>
> *And next he took his little heir,*
> *Oh, most unnat'ral father!*
> *And flung it out of a two pair*
> *Window; for he'd rather*
>
> *Possess the lady of his love,*
> *Than lady of the law, Sir,*
> *And car'd not for his child above*
> *A pinch of Maccabau, Sir.*[19]

A newspaper account of a Punch and Judy show dated September 22, 1813, describes the rest of the story as follows:

The dead bodies having been found, police officers enter the dwelling of Mr. Punch, who flies for his life, mounts his steed, and the author, neglecting, like other great poets, the confining unities of time and place, conveys his hero into Spain, where, however, he is arrested by an officer of the terrible Inquisition. After enduring the most cruel tortures with incredible fortitude, Mr. Punch, by means of a golden key (a beautiful and novel allegory), opens his prison door and escapes. The conclusion of the affecting story is satirical, allegorical, and poetical. The hero is first overtaken by weariness and laziness in the shape of a black dog whom he fights and conquers; disease, in the disguise of a physician, next arrests him; but Punch "sees through the thin pre-

---

[19] Cited in J. P. Collier, *Punch and Judy* (New York: Rimington and Hooper, 1929), pp. 56–58.

tense" and dismisses the doctor with a few derogatory kicks. Death at length visits the fugitive, but Punch lays about his skeleton carcass so lustily and makes the bones of his antagonist rattle so musically with a bastinado *that "Death his death's blow then received." Last of all comes the Devil; first, under the appearance of a lovely female, but afterward in his own natural shape, to drag the offender to the infernal regions, in purgatory to expiate his dreadful crimes. Even this attempt fails, and Punch is left triumphant over Doctors, Death, and the Devil. The curtain falls amid the shouts of the Conqueror, who on his victorious staff lifts on high his vanquished foe.*[20]

In *Jack and the Beanstalk,* the giant would kill Jack. In some of the versions we have the giant saying,

> *Fee fie fo fum,*
> *I smell the blood of an Englishman.*
> *Be he alive or be he dead*
> *I'll grind his bones to make my bread.*

We have here what may be an allusion to one of the most archaic of myths, the story of Adam and Eve as written in the Bible. Adam and Eve are depicted eating of the tree of knowledge. I was once told that the fruit of the tree of "knowledge"—knowledge also being the biblical authors' word for sexual intercourse—was a baby. If this interpretation has any validity, then it is fitting that consequent upon the sin of eating this fruit, both must become modest. The punishments are pain for Eve in childbirth and for Adam condemnation to a vegetable diet. He is to eat "the herb of the field, in the sweat of thy face shalt thou eat *bread.*" Jack's potential killer would grind into the bread the fruit of the tree of knowledge.

The cannibalistic theme with respect to children is

[20] Collier, pp. 67–69.

70

barely disguised in the fairy-tale literature. The witch, the giant, the bear, and the wolf eat children. The child as the target of the cannibalistic tendency is represented very clearly in the *Gingerbread Man,* who must keep running in order not to be eaten. And in Lewis Carroll's Alice story, we have the child turning into a little pig, which, of course, is a license to the imagination to think of the child as to be eaten. The story of the *Three Little Pigs* is basically the story of three little children put out at an early age to fend for themselves and is thus similar to *Hansel and Gretel.* The three little pigs are principally potential items of diet for the wolf, who huffs and puffs and then devours them—at least the ones who can not defend themselves. The triumph of the third pig is that he can cook the wolf. In the Bible, in the archetypal sacrifice story of Abraham and Isaac, the edible ram replaces Isaac. In another story in the Bible, less well known, two women, together under siege, each have a child and agree to have a joint meal out of one of the children on one day and another meal out of the other child on the next day.[21]

The theme of cannibalism is not so lost even among the children of modern affluent society as not to make the cat-and-mouse chase, the cat seeking to eat the mouse (with the mouse clearly the young child), one of the most popular themes for the contemporary cartoon movie. *Tom and Jerry* is basically the same story as *Jack and the Beanstalk,* with Tom seeking to eat Jerry and Jerry managing to escape. It is also the same as the *Hansel and Gretel* story. The tempting candy house that the children nibble on is akin to the piece of cheese placed outside the mouse hole to tempt Jerry to come out. In the fairy tale, the child gets deep satisfaction from the children's triumph in this conflict. The story reflects the child's sense of danger—the feeling that he will be victimized, literally killed and eaten, by people older than

[21] 2 Kings 6:26.

71

he. The fact that these stories characteristically end with the triumph of the child makes it possible for them to reveal the great fears in the mind of the child. One of his chief urges is to grow up, to be so large and so strong that he will not be the target of the hostile wishes of those who are older and larger than he is.

Because of the child's sense of being victimized and because of his identification with animals, the purveyors of fictional materials for consumption by children have a cardinal rule not to show an animal being killed. It horrifies children too much, for it comes too close to the real condition in their minds. Thus, it is perfectly all right, for example, to show battle scenes with human beings being slaughtered by the hundreds and by the thousands. It is perfectly all right to show children scenes of men being mutilated, tortured, shot, and killed. But one dare not show the slaughter of a pig in an abattoir. The latter has a realism for the child that cannot easily be defended against. The normal repressive mechanisms are simply inadequate to cope with it.

Children are not free of hostility, however. Freud shocked people by smashing the myth of the innocence of children. He pointed out that one could, if one looked deeply into a child's unconscious, find a wish on the part of the child to destroy the parent. However, since the parent is the stronger of the two and since, if the child expresses his homicidal impulse, it leads to retaliation, the child must repress the hostile wish.

In my opinion Freud's point is correct, but only partially correct. That there is such a wish, particularly strong in children with some kind of disturbance and to a lesser degree in healthy children, is perhaps not to be denied. However, a deeper question is involved: Whence comes this wish? Is it, as Freud so strongly suggested, simply the result of being a child, simply something constitutional, as it were? Or, perhaps, is it not the result of the child's already appreciating, albeit unconsciously, the hostile impulses against

72

himself? The story which Freud took as the paradigm, the story of Oedipus, begins with the father, Laius, putting the infant Oedipus out to die. The first aggressive impulse is of the father against Oedipus. Unfortunately, in most of Freud's writings on the Oedipus complex, he tended to ignore the first part of the Greek story. Yet he did not ignore it completely. In discussing some case material, he wrote:

My patient's father had the characteristic, shown by so many people in relation to their children, of indulging in "affectionate abuse"; and it is possible that during the patient's earlier years his father . . . may more than once, as he caressed the little boy or played with him, have threatened in fun to "gobble him up." One of my patients told me that her two children could never get to be fond of their grandfather because in the course of his affectionate romping with them he used to frighten them by saying he would cut open their tummies![22]

Affectionate abuse of this kind is reflected in some of the classical riddle rhymes:

> *When I went up Sandy-Hill*
> *I met a sandy-boy;*
> *I cut his throat, I sucked his blood,*
> *And left his skin a-hanging-o.*[23]

The threat is removed from this rhyme when it is revealed that it refers to an orange. Another example refers to currants:

> *Higgledy-piggledy*
> *Here we be,*

[22] S. Freud, *Collected Papers,* Vol. 3, A. Strachey and J. Strachey (Trans.) (London: Hogarth, 1900), p. 302.
[23] Cited in Opie and Opie, p. 207.

Slaughter of the Innocents

Picked and plucked,
And put in a pie.[24]

Does the child "know" all that I ascribe to his appreciation of the stories he enjoys so much? In the simplest sense of the word *know* he does not. That is, questioning of even an articulate child is not likely to elicit the understanding I am suggesting. Even further, the very innocence of the child in this respect is perhaps one of his greatest defenses. "Though he slay me, yet will I trust him" (Job 13:15) is virtually a perfect description of the state of mind of the child, at least of the child who stands a chance of survival against a strong infanticidal impulse in an adult. To make this clear, I have to point out that the person who engages in infanticide tends to ascribe a greater level of maturity to the child than that which exists. In particular, he attributes greater willfulness and intention to do malice than the child may often even be capable of. Thus, for example, he may talk of the wickedness and the naughtiness that the child displayed in soiling itself. Such a person is, in effect, attributing a control over defecation that the infant simply does not have. The attribution of wicked intent to the child thus is associated with a license to abuse the child. But a clear lack of such intention on the part of the child is a protection.

To put this explanation another way, there is a built-in mechanism in most human beings to have their anger turned off by innocence. The child, for example, has broken something or has dumped a glass of milk over the floor. This provokes anger and irritation. And then the child does something imperfect. That is important. The imperfection which we respond to as cute—being cute and being imperfect are often virtually the same—turns off the anger. A biologist has suggested to me that he thinks that this mechanism is one which has been positively selected by evolution. We may

[24] Cited in Opie and Opie, p. 377.

suppose that children have varied in the degree to which they display the characteristic of cuteness. In the long evolutionary process, those who were more cute tended to survive and to transmit cuteness in childhood to the next generation. Those who were born less cute stood a lower chance of surviving through infancy and childhood. In addition, parents who thus had their anger turned off equally were winners in the propagation history of the world.

One of the defenses that the child has is his very innocence, his very lack of understanding of the fact that there may be hostile impulses toward him. Should he too quickly become conscious, he may act in such a way as to defend himself, placing himself in a battle in which he is literally not equal. Instead, he is better off, as it were, saying in his own way, "Though he slay me, yet will I trust him." We are again brought back to the Garden of Eden myth. As the child grows even slightly out of innocence into sophistication, he must deal and cope with the message "revealed unto babes."

One way of dealing with abuse is to run away, a common fantasy. The fairy-story literature is replete with young people wandering about the world by themselves without the help or care of older people. This fantasy of independence from adults arises in part because the dependency the child experiences is not adequately satisfied.

The fantasy of growth is another common way for the child to cope with the sense that there are hostile adults. The child imagines himself as somehow out of the children's stage of life. Thus, for example, *Jack and the Beanstalk* relates increasing competence on the part of Jack. In the beginning a rather inadequate young Jack is so stupid that he sells a cow for a handful of beans. But in the end Jack is competent, crafty, and wealthy; in the course of the story he has changed into a man.

A common female fantasy, represented in many fairy tales, is the growth of the girl to a point where she is attractive and mature enough to be saved from mistreating adults by a rich and princely lover who may awaken her out of her sexual unresponsiveness, represented by sleep, to her maturity, by a kiss. Or, she may grow so much that her prince comes up the tower on her long hair, a representation of sexual maturity.

An extremely common fantasy for a child is the so-called family romance, the fantasy that his parents are not really his parents but that he is, in one way or another, a stepchild. The child essentially solves the riddle of his victimization by his parents by not allowing them to be his legitimate parents, thereby answering the message that he has received from their abuse—the message that he is not quite legitimate and that he does not have a valid claim on life. In real life this fantasy occurs among children with a very high frequency. In the children's stories it is found in the repeated idea that the actual parents of the child are not alive. In *Hansel and Gretel, Cinderella, Snow White*, and even *Pinocchio,* the parents are not biological parents. And often, in one way or another, a dead mother comes out of the grave to provide for and protect a neglected or abused child. The family romance is clearly depicted in *The Ugly Duckling*. The young "duckling" is hatched with other ducklings but is not one of them, and it turns out later that he is a swan. The basic pattern of identification is of the child with the duckling. The family in which he immediately finds himself is not the real one; somehow, somewhere, there is to be found his real family.

The family romance is also found in the history of religious thought in the idea of God. Thus, one of the important functions of God is to act as the real parent, in the absence of a satisfactory parent in the flesh. In *Hansel and Gretel,* when the two children are alone in the woods, having been abandoned by the parents, Gretel is frightened. Hansel tries to comfort her and tells her not to worry because "God will not forsake us." One possible psychological explanation of the idea of the virgin birth is as the extreme and ultimate fulfillment of the family romance—the only true father is the father who is in heaven.

Thus, much is revealed unto babes in the literature for children. The themes of the literature help the child to cope with eternal problems of being. Some of these problems are rooted in the essential features of human existence, such as the great dependence of the child on the favor of adults.

FOUR

~~~~~~~~~~~~~~~~~~~~~~~~~~~~~~

One Less
Mouth to Feed

~~~~~~~~~~~~~~~~~~~~~~~~~~~~~~

In this and the next chapter I attempt to round out the hypothesis which was earlier stated that the problem of child abuse is to be understood in the context of the larger problem of the balance of resources and population. Child abuse may be meaningfully classified as one among the several checks on population that Malthus was concerned with. However, to avoid misinterpretation some disclaimers must be made. Unfortunately, some of the contemporary discussions on the question of population suffer from over-simplification, conceiving of it in terms of so-called population density and giving too little consideration to the human organism as a producer of resources in addition to being a consumer of them. When we consider the population prob-

78

lem with respect to human beings, density, as such, should not be considered with respect to space, as is commonly done, but rather with respect to the resources which are needed to live. Density in the city is greater than density in the country, and yet it is possible to live eminently comfortably in the city, usually more comfortably than in the country. Whereas the population density of China is about two hundred persons per square mile, the density of the Netherlands is about one thousand persons per square mile, with a substantially higher average standard of living. At times it has been advantageous to increase population density considerably because of the way in which that density helps in the creation of resources.

What I have said in the above paragraph is to forestall any interpretation of what I present in this and the next chapter as a belief that child abuse is natural and that therefore nothing is to be done about it. At the present time we are in one of the greatest periods of growth of the powers of man to enlarge resources for living. It may indeed be possible in the future to tolerate human densities on the earth of a kind that have hardly been imagined before if we learn how to provide resources. Human beings, in their creation of resources, characteristically produce goods or services. However, one of the most important services rendered by human beings entails care for the young. In a society in which less human energy may be required for the development of the goods needed for life, a greater proportion of human energy can be devoted to the care of the young. Thus, if the balance between the number of people and the goods available for living becomes unproblematical, the problem of balance of resources becomes largely the problem of the balance between those who care for others and those needing care.

We must be prepared to believe that the current condition of mankind in the universe is an early stage of evolution and that as the role of natural mechanisms decreases, evolution will increasingly give a role to the intelligence of man. Man, with his intelligence, must then comprehend the natural mechanisms to which he is heir and must use his intelligence to make nature more humane.

BIOLOGICAL MECHANISMS AND CONSCIOUSNESS

Most biological mechanisms are not under the control of conscious processes, yet many mechanisms may be mediated through conscious processes. Thus, for example, the biological need for food may be mediated through conscious hunger in organisms which have consciousness. However, food-getting takes place among living forms that do not have a hunger mechanism. Moreover, a biological mechanism may be mediated by consciousness in many ways. Thus the regulation of population is not necessarily a conscious function on the part of the individuals who engage in actions that result in such regulation. Whatever individual motives and biological and psychological dynamics there may be, population regulation tends to result. As Sumner aptly puts it:

All the folkways which go to make up a population policy seem to imply greater knowledge of the philosophy of population than can be ascribed to uncivilized men. The case is one, however, in which knowledge is simple and the acts proceed from immediate interest, while the generalization is an unapprehended result. The mothers know the strain of child-bearing and child-rearing. They refuse to undergo it for purely egoistic reasons. The consequent adjustment of the population to the food supply comes of itself. It was never foreseen or purposed by anybody. . . . Abortion and infanticide are primary and violent acts of self-defense by the parents against famine, disease, and other calamities of overpopulation, which increase with the number which each man or woman has to provide for.[1]

[1] W. G. Sumner, *Folkways* (Boston: Ginn, 1906), pp. 312–313.

80

One Less Mouth to Feed

Erik H. Erikson, in his *Childhood and Society*,[2] brings considerable weight to the thesis that parents, in the practices they engage in when rearing their children, produce individuals whose traits satisfy the needs of the total society. At the same time the parents may not do this wittingly. The Sioux mother may have had no idea, for example, that her particular style of nursing her infant son was likely to produce a certain type of courageous warrior.

Infanticide must be regarded as a property of the social collective. Emile Durkheim interprets suicide as the manifestation of "the collective affection from which we suffer."[3] And, indeed, child abuse and suicide may not be very far apart. Durkheim found and many studies since his have confirmed that psychosocial isolation is a critical factor in suicide, and it appears to be a factor in child abuse also. A remarkably large number of families in which child abuse has occurred have few ties to the community. The families are typically anomic and alienated, virtually isolated, without friends or interested relatives, without religious affiliation, and without any club or group membership or association.[4]

A comprehensive demographic study of child abuse has not yet been made,[5] but, from our experience with numerous other similar and related phenomena, such as crime, demographic relationships will undoubtedly emerge when such studies are made. The occurrence of phenomena with

[2] E. H. Erikson, *Childhood and Society* (New York: Norton, 1963).

[3] E. Durkheim, *Suicide: A Study in Sociology*, J. A. Spaulding and G. Simpson (Trans.) (New York: Free Press, 1951), p. 37.

[4] V. J. Fontana, D. Donovan, and R. T. Wong, "The 'Maltreatment Syndrome' in Children," *New England Journal of Medicine*, 1963, *269*, 1389. S. M. Nurse, "Familial Patterns of Parents Who Abuse Their Children," *Smith College Studies in Social Work*, 1964, *35*, 24–25.

[5] The best we have to date is D. Gil, "Incidence of Child Abuse and Demographic Characteristics of Persons Involved," in R. E. Helfer and C. H. Kempe (Eds.), *The Battered Child* (Chicago: Chicago University Press, 1968), pp. 19–42. But as Gil himself indicates, the limited available data allow only very tentative assertions.

certain regularities indicates that social forces tend to create the phenomena. Thus, much of what we have learned from and since Durkheim suggests, for example, that the number of cases of child abuse within a given demographical unit does not vary very substantially from year to year and is subject to some trend influences. In discussing the presumptive force that creates the regularity, Durkheim says, "Such a force does not determine one individual rather than another. It exacts a definite number of certain kinds of actions, but not that they should be performed by this or that person. It may be granted that some people resist the force, and it has its way with others."[6] The understanding of phenomena of this order is not to be achieved exclusively in terms of "individual factors . . . temperament, character, antecedents, and private history."[7] Durkheim's perspective can be brought together with the psychoanalytic perspective which views the essential psychodynamic mechanisms as the same in the normal and the abnormal personality. The psychoanalysts, by focusing their attention not on the frankly psychotic but on the neurotic, were able to identify what may be regarded as genotypic identities in all human personality, leaving gross differences in manifest behavior as phenotypic differences. Indeed, the psychoanalytic school can allow itself to entertain the grossest "sins" in thought, conscious or unconscious, almost because they recognize simultaneously that a sin in thought is not necessarily the same as the sin in deed. For example, all children, even all people, may harbor unconscious and repressed incest wishes. However, it is very far from this kind of incest to real incest. Indeed, one could well make out a case that it is possible to consider incest wishes precisely because they are repressed and not acted out in behavior, paradoxical as it may appear to be.

[6] Durkheim, p. 325.
[7] Durkheim, p. 46.

NATURAL POPULATION CONTROL MECHANISMS

A number of mechanisms in animals may be conceived as natural population control mechanisms. The most obvious check on population is the death rate. However, a number of studies have shown that the mechanisms for the death of organisms not only are resident in external factors such as war and food shortages but also are genetically carried by the organism. Through endocrinal mechanisms of the kind identified by Hans Selye, organisms respond to negative environmental factors. Thus, "if . . . food shortages, climatic catastrophes, and disease . . . do not limit population growth, then density-dependent behavioral endocrine mechanisms will."[8]

Among animals, the rate of hepatitis rises in deer as the density of deer increases in an area.[9] Renal diseases among woodchucks[10] increase as the density of woodchucks increases. Conditions of crowding inhibit sexual maturation. Under inappropriate conditions, as in zoos, animals refrain from copulation. Some animal studies show that crowding results in a decrease in testicular weight in males and fewer implantations.[11] Crowding among drosophila reduces the number of eggs laid by the females. Among rodents crowding results in reduced lactation among the mothers, carelessness in nursing, desertion of the young, and even eating of the young. There is a decrease of survival rate from

---

[8] J. J. Christian, "The Pathology of Overpopulation," *Military Medicine,* 1963, *128,* 572. Christian's thought in this quotation is conditioned by studies of animals, in which there is a high correlation between density and resources simply because animals do not do very much to increase the resources for themselves in the way that human beings do. However, if we substitute "population-resource balance" for "density-dependent" in this quotation, we may generalize to humans.

[9] Christian, p. 592.
[10] Christian, p. 599.
[11] Christian, pp. 576, 585.

birth to weaning.[12] In some organisms there is an increase of the resorption of embryos[13] and generally greater intrauterine mortality.[14]

Among humans, the virtually universal tendency to refrain from engaging in sexual relations in the sight of a third party may be identified as a population control mechanism. This mechanism is directly related to the degree of crowding since the more crowding there is the less likely it is that sexual relations may be unobserved.[15] The very custom, virtually universal, of keeping the genitalia covered works toward the control of population. I would speculate that as we increase our ability to control fertility by reliable contraception, the tendency to keep the genitalia covered will probably decrease radically. Just as the covering of the genitalia is a universal signal to discourage sexual advances, the removal of clothing is an invitation. Burlesque dancers and the like are most successful in their aim by providing the sight of the removal of clothing, rather than the simple exhibition of nakedness. As has been suggested, the story of eating from the tree of knowledge is an injunction to keep the population down through modesty, the covering of the genitalia, rather than through the destruction of children. The ease with which young females may be traumatized by rough initial sexual experiences, creating an aversion to further sexual contacts, may be viewed as a population-controlling mechanism. And certainly every contrasexual ideological or moral position is, in this sense, contraceptive.

Incest taboos, which are universal, are equally a mechanism that is functionally population-controlling. In-

---

[12] Christian, p. 579.

[13] Christian, p. 576.

[14] Christian, p. 581.

[15] Again, crowding should not be identified simply with density as measured for example, by the number of persons per unit of surface. An apartment house in a large city has a high density per unit of surface but may not be crowded at all.

cest taboos keep sex partners who are most accessible to each other apart. They restrict population by channeling sexual interest away from the available to less available strangers who are not of the immediate family. If one may not have sexual intercourse except with someone from a distant village, fewer pregnancies occur.

Sexual perversions, in providing alternative sexual outlets, characteristically work to keep population down. Sexual perversions usually occur with greater frequency among males than among females. Sexual deviation among females often manifests itself in promiscuity. However, forms of polyandry, among which we must count female promiscuity and prostitution, keep population down by reducing the proportion of copulations with fertile females.

The unique relationship between menstruation and fertility in the human species may be the result of evolution as it has produced population-restraining mechanisms. In many nonhuman mammals the heat period is near the time of ovulation and thus encourages fertilization. In the human female, the data suggest that the period of maximum sexual responsiveness is just prior to the onset of menstruation.[16] This is, however, a period of low fertility. Thus, for human beings the temporal pattern of female sexual interest is in the direction of the restriction of population.[17]

Perhaps the most significant mechanism for the control of population is the extreme vulnerability and relative lack of viability of the human infant. The ease with which a human child can die may be regarded as a test. The newborn child comes into life, testing, as it were, the immediate

[16] A. C. Kinsey, W. B. Pomeroy, C. E. Martin, and P. H. Gebhard, *Sexual Behavior in the Human Female* (Philadelphia: Saunders, 1953), p. 609.

[17] I have heard this used as an argument by some Catholics to favor the use of contraception. The remainder of the argument is that if contraception is thus natural, as the discrepancy between the time of fertility and sexual interest seems to be, then other forms of contraception should equally be viewed as natural.

environment for fitness. If it is unfit, he retires quickly into nonexistence. Even under such conditions for the care of infants as prevail in the United States, the greatest death rate is in the first year of life. And even within the first year, more than two-thirds of those deaths occur in the first four weeks. In fact, more infants die in the first four weeks than in any year-long age group. Infant mortality certainly remains high. However, we must not overlook the fact that modern medicine has done a great deal in eliminating at least certain causes of death of infants. Perhaps the step taken by those associated with modern medicine toward opening up the question of child-abuse—and we must remember that the medical profession played a critical role in this—is the logical one for them after the conquest of many of the diseases of childhood.

As we consider the varieties of ways in which population has been controlled and include infant mortality among them, we must also recognize a genre of consolation literature which was of considerable magnitude and which aimed at helping parents by reconciling them to the death of children.

> *Before thy heart had learn'd*
> *In waywardness to stray,*
> *Before thy feet had turn'd*
> *The dark and downward way.*
> *Ere sin had sear'd the breast,*
> *Or sorrow woke the tear;*
> *Rise to thy home of rest,*
> *In yon celestial sphere.*[18]

Or,

Weeping mother! is it not a balsam to your bleeding heart

[18] L. H. S., "On Seeing an Infant Prepared for the Grave," *The Mother's Magazine*, April 1833, p. 66.

to believe that your infant child now rests in the bosom of that Savior who, when on earth, exclaimed, "Suffer little children," etc. So that you may now say over its sleeping body, smiling in its sweet repose, "It is well with the child." That infant mind which here on earth was folded up like a bud expands and blooms in the light and warmth of heaven. It drinks in the pleasures of a rational, holy, and immortal existence.

In many respects it must be wiser than any sage on earth. It is the companion of angels; it has seen God and his son Jesus Christ. It hath entered before you on its exalted career. While you are left to struggle longer with doubt and danger, that infant child has spread its wings for its upward flight, nearer and nearer to the throne. You have a new relationship to heaven. There your offspring dwell. Surely you must discern a new and peculiar meaning in the beautiful words of the Psalmist—"Lo, children are a heritage of the Lord; happy is the man that hath his quiver full of them."[19]

The theme in the Old Testament that the firstborn child belongs to God has an interesting biological confirmation. The young infant tests the environment, as it were, not only for physical suitability but also to determine whether the world is prepared to care for him. The test is greatest, from a statistical point of view, for the woman who has never had a child before, as, in the context of such evolutionary thought, it "should be." The average weight of newborn infants is directly related to the birth rank of the child, with firstborns characteristically lowest in weight, secondborns higher. Since the probability of surviving is directly related to the baby's weight at birth, this tests the readiness of the mother and her physical and social situation for tak-

[19] W. A., "On the Death of Infants," *The Mother's Magazine*, May 1834, p. 76.

ing care of the child. If a mother can manage to keep a child of slight weight alive, it attests to her mother readiness. If conditions are such that she is less ready to provide for the child, then the child is more likely to die. The death rate for firstborns is substantially higher than for secondborns, although it rises again for laterborns,[20] probably as a function of demands on resources including those necessary for parenting a large family.

Positing infanticide as a natural form of adaptation poses some difficulty in connection with the ordinarily maintained view of the nature of evolution as this has come to us from Darwin from the middle of the nineteenth century. To suggest that the killing of one's own offspring is adaptive raises the question of how such a trait may be transmitted if indeed the very offspring are killed. To solve this problem we need to recognize a limitation of the Darwinian notion. The Darwinian view of the evolutionary process tends to look at each individual organism separately and conceives of its adaptation or failure of adaptation to the environment as the chief locus for the operation of the principle of natural selection. According to the Darwinian view, individual organisms possessing successful adjustment mechanisms survive and transmit these successful adjustment mechanisms to their offspring. Advances to the theory of evolution have added a correction which is important for appreciating child abuse in such an evolutionary context. Natural selection works not only through the adjustment mechanisms of the individual organism but through groups of organisms. Group survival is more important than individual survival to the biological history of the species. Thus mechanisms that serve the interests of the group and of the species are passed on

[20] J. Loeb, *Weight at Birth and Survival of New-Born, by age of Mother and Total-Birth Order: United States, Early 1950,* Selected Studies, Vol. 47, No. 2, August 6, 1958. Bethesda, Md.: National Office of Vital Statistics, Department of Health, Education and Welfare.

through generations.[21] Mechanisms that are individually maladaptive may be positively selected providing they serve species survival. Individual organisms are thus possessed of individually maladaptive mechanisms which serve the species as a whole. Critical instances are those mechanisms which reduce population density if that density is maladaptive for the species. A main difference between the two views of evolution is in connection with the death of individual organisms. Whereas death has always been something of an enigma to classical evolutionary theory, in the more recent view the fact that an individual organism must die may be viewed as serving the purpose of the survival of the species and is itself a trait cultivated by the evolutionary process, given the need for new organisms to manifest the variation that the process of natural selection itself requires.

CHILDHOOD HELPLESSNESS AND PARENTAL SACRIFICE

To return to the underlying biological situation with respect to child abuse, an essential feature is the very helplessness of children; rather great resources are required for the maintenance of children quite beyond the resources required for most other organisms. Child abuse is the antithesis of child care, with the need for child care creating the possibility of child abuse. Because this need for caring for the child may constitute an injury to parents, the impulse to kill the child arises as a defense against the threat associated with the demand for caring for him. Child abuse should be understood as a reaction to the strains of parenthood. Although certain natural forces may be conducive to making parents care for their children, nonetheless there must be adequate contextual supports for the parents in this enterprise. In the relative absence of social support, one may ex-

[21] V. C. Wynne-Edwards, *Animal Dispersion in Relation to Social Behaviour* (New York: Hafner, 1962).

pect that contrary impulses arise, even if they are not always acted out.

It has sometimes been speculated that poverty is the major cause of infanticide and that the frustrations of poverty or lower social class are associated with child abuse. In individual cases it is hard to reject the notion that poverty must play some role. Where there is a tenuous equilibrium with respect to needs, including needs for food, clothing, shelter, and space, and where there are arduous demands for labor and attention to maintain these needs, then it would appear that poverty is a variable in infanticide or child abuse. The data currently available do not, however, indicate a relationship between child abuse and social or economic levels.[22] It is probably better to look into the way in which the coming of the child tends to disturb the total equilibrium of the life of the parents, including the possibility of the child's creating disturbances in the sexual sphere, the social sphere, the occupational sphere, and the total income of the adult, not only of material things but of such things as "esteem income," to borrow a concept from Robert White.[23] For human beings the social competition may not be strictly in terms of food supply, as Malthus tended to think of it, but more generally in terms of the way in which, given the specific cultural contexts as well as the biological context, children constitute a burden calling for sacrifices on the part of the adult population.

The helplessness of the child may be the stimulus for engaging in child abuse by parents who themselves are overwhelmed by feelings of helplessness. Commenting on the relationship between the needs of the family as a whole and the likelihood of battering a child, one psychiatrist says:

[22] S. R. Zalba, "The Abused Child. I. A Survey of the Problem," *Social Work*, 1966, *11* (4), 6.

[23] R. W. White, *The Abnormal Personality* (2nd ed.) (New York: Ronald, 1956), p. 61.

90

It's almost as though love is like a bag of jelly beans, a limited supply, and, at a critical time (when the supply is low for the entire family), along comes a stranger and puts his hand out for more than his share. This is the way that the baby is often viewed. There are many things that can make this the particular time when the bag of jelly beans is depleted for the family. We must remember that even in normal families, pregnancy, motherhood, fatherhood can be viewed as chronic stress situations. There are changes in role, personality maturation problems, and new sacrifices that are called forth each time a new baby comes. Particularly in a family where some members are feeling very deprived, feeling that the child is taking more of the wife's attention or husband's money, this is often a time when the child gets battered.[24]

Sumner succinctly cited two reasons for infanticide, ego and misery.

Children add to the weight of the struggle for existence of their parents. The relation of parent to child is one of sacrifice. The interests of children and parents are antagonistic. The fact that there are or may be compensations does not affect the primary relation between the two. It may well be believed that if procreation had not been put under the dominion of a great passion, it would have been caused to cease by the burdens it entails. Abortion and infanticide are especially interesting because they show how early in the history of civilization the burden of children became so heavy that parents began to shirk it and also because they show the rise of a population policy, which is one of the most important programs of practical expediency which any society ever can adopt.[25]

[24] I. D. Milowe, cited in K. Bain and others, "Child Abuse and Injury," *Military Medicine*, 1965, *130*, 750–751.
[25] Sumner, pp. 309–310.

When the women's rights movement in America was particularly strident, the psychologist Leta Hollingworth wrote: "The bearing and rearing of children is painfully dangerous to life and involves long years of exacting labor and self-sacrifice."[26] Although she did not deny that women may have a desire for children, she indicated that social pressure over and above any natural desire for children is necessary to get women to submit to these dangers and sacrifices.

The acceptance of the parental role characteristically entails a radical modification in the total style of life of the mother and father. In almost every society the change to parenthood entails a change in social status. Sometimes it involves an enhancement of the status, but often it may not. Children also characteristically restrain physical movement, with the caretaker of the child being bound to the place where the child is located since, if the child is abandoned for any length of time, it perishes, and travel with children in the absence of appropriate equipment is very difficult. When Watson sought to find the stimulus initially bound to the anger response, he identified restraint of movement as its major instigator,[27] and we may suspect that the anger of a parent toward a child is in some way related to this primitive stimulus of anger. The necessities of child care dictate rather precisely the kinds of activity that one must engage in and the amount of attention, time, and energy to devote to these activities.

The psychological obstacles in the path of growing into the acceptance of the parental role are numerous and include all the things which the psychoanalysts regard as obstacles toward attaining genitality. Helene Deutsch, in her sensitive treatment of the psychology of motherhood, says:

[26] L. S. Hollingworth, "Social Devices for Impelling Women to Bear and Rear Children," *American Journal of Sociology*, 1916, 22, 20–21.

[27] J. B. Watson, *Psychology from the Standpoint of a Behaviorist* (Philadelphia: Lippincott, 1919).

The psychologic difficulty that stands in the way of direct realization of motherhood can have various causes; their most frequent common denominator is woman's fear of losing her personality in favor of the child. This fear may manifest itself as primitive fear of death or as concern over the threatened erotic values and physical beauty; it may derive from the fear of real obligations and restrictions through pregnancy, etc.; it is often an oppressive fear of the loss of professional and intellectual values or a feeling of insufficiency with regard to the great emotional demands of motherhood. All these and many other fears, often justified, are based upon the natural law that the old must yield to the new. . . . The wisdom of nature has provided means for conquering them. Woman's love for her child is normally greater than her self-love, and the idea of eternity inherent in reproduction overcomes her fear of being destroyed. The future triumphs over the present, but only if the past is favorably disposed of.[28]

Over and above such particular facts as the loss of beauty and sexual attractiveness, the loss of physical mobility, and the demands on the resources of food, there is the general factor that children may interfere with the personal aims of parents. It will always remain true, as Sumner says, that "the able bodied and competent part of a society is the adults in the prime of life. These have to bear all of the societal burdens, among which are the care of those too young and of those too old to care for themselves."[29]

Earlier the question was raised as to whether and in what sense there may be a natural tendency toward infanticide. One can just as readily ask whether and in what sense there may be a natural tendency toward child care. There is,

[28] H. Deutsch, *Psychology of Women.* Vol. 2. *Motherhood* (New York: Grune and Stratton, 1945), p. 47.
[29] Sumner, p. 308.

93

in fact, a most interesting contrast between the literature of sentiment and the psychological literature on human motivation. The literature of sentiment celebrates the deep love of parents for children, but actual evidence is not too available. A desire for progeny or an impulse to care for the young has not impressed most students of human motivation. Characteristically, other motives are stressed, and care for progeny is, at best, seen as a by-product of other motivational factors, rather than an original motivational aim in any sense. No contemporary school of thought within the social sciences has been especially impressed by the idea that the care of children is particularly significant for appreciating the human condition, even though the continued existence of the species is clearly contingent on the way in which man cares for his children. This dearth reflects something about both the nature of man and the sciences of man and likely relates to our earlier considerations of the silence in history about child abuse and infanticide.

In my searches I have been able to find little concern with the human desire for progeny except in two psychological systems, psychoanalysis and phrenology, both of which have been the object of seriously discrediting criticism. There is the classic psychoanalytic treatment of motherhood by Deutsch,[30] which I have already discussed. The phrenologists identified a separate psychological factor for love of children, philoprogenitiveness. J. G. Spurzheim, the leading systematist of the school, indicated it was necessary to create a word for it because none existed in the English language:

As the English language possesses no single word that indicates love of offspring, I have employed two Greek roots which, in conjunction, define accurately the primitive propensity. The title that results is long; but I could not say

---

[30] Deutsch, *Psychology of Women.*

94

*philogenitiveness because that would indicate the love of
producing offspring. As, however, progeny is synonymous
with offspring and philoprogeny means the love of offspring,
I adopt the term philoprogenitiveness for the faculty of producing the love of offspring.*[31]

Some of the observations of the phrenological school
are worthy of attention. The phrenological school may be
considered to have made three contributions to the history
of psychology,[32] two of them sound. The unsound idea is
that protuberances on the brain and the skull are simply
related to specific psychological functions. The sound ones
are that the brain is significant to the nature of psychological
functioning and that there are pronounced differences from
individual to individual in psychological functions. Spurzheim was very aware of the enormous variation that existed
with respect to philoprogenitiveness. There are enormous
differences from species to species in the degree to which
animals take care of their progeny. Generally, females appear to be "more energetic,"[33] as he put it, than males in the
degree to which they are attached to and tend to the needs
of their offspring. But, even beyond such gross differences,
a great deal of variation still exists:

*Among all kinds of animals which take care of their progeny,
there are always some females who feel little or none of the
propensity, and certain males who manifest the inclination
strongly. There are even women who look on children as a
heavy burden, though the majority deem them their chief
treasure and greatest source of happiness; and this is not
only in the miserable portion of society, but indiscriminately*

[31] J. G. Spurzheim, *Phrenology* (Philadelphia: Lippincott, 1908),
p. 179.

[32] See D. Bakan, "The Influence of Phrenology on American Psychology," *Journal of the History of the Behavioral Science,* 1966, *2,* 200–220.

[33] Spurzheim, p. 176.

among the rich and poor. Cases of insanity are by no means unfrequent in which the function of parental love is deranged.[34]

Childbirth itself is perhaps the paradigmatic instance of injury to the parent on account of the child. Here we have a severe and unambiguous example of the way in which the reproductive process may work against the individual interests of the organism. Indeed, as some thought in evolutionary theory suggests, reproduction always entails some sacrifice on the part of the parent organism, and this very sacrificial trait has been the product of natural selection.[35] This observation again suggests the profundity and distillation of experience contained in the Garden of Eden story. Childbirth involves literal injury to the mother and great pain, although strong social forces would make us want to put this pain out of mind. Thus, the experience of childbirth may well arouse aggressive impulses in the mother toward the child. This aggression may not be unique either to very painful and exhausting deliveries or to young mothers, although these factors may enhance the aggression. The fact is that human children are not born without jeopardy and at least temporary injury to the mother. Poisoning, increased varicosity of veins, and literal tissue injury are common accompaniments of pregnancy. If one were seeking some regular biological event with which to identify original sin, it would not be the child's urge to kill his father, as Freud might have suggested, but the pain and injury of every child to his mother in pregnancy and parturition. The mother literally suffers that the child shall live. The Christian association of pain and compassion is profoundly rooted in the human psychological condition. The pain of childbirth has the effect, when the mechanism is working properly, to sen-

[34] Spurzheim, p. 177.
[35] G. C. Williams, *Adaptation and Natural Selection* (Princeton, N.J.: Princeton University Press, 1966), p. 26.

sitize the mother to the cries of pain and discomfort that the child emits and results in her having compassion for the child. A mutuality between the pain of the mother and the pain of the child unites them and preserves the latter.

The mortality of women caused by complications of pregnancy and childbirth stands as evidence that the jeopardy is, in fact, quite real. Even after a successful delivery, postpartum aggressions toward the child may well be exacerbated by the inordinate demands that child care makes. Deutsch points out that "in our culture, after a very painful and exhausting delivery, the young mother's anxiety and aggression are intensified."[36]

If she is aggressive two options are open. She can direct aggression to the husband, the first cause, or to the child, the second. Needing the babying herself and fearing the aggression of the male and sometimes feeling also her loss of sexual attractiveness, she may divert the aggression toward the child. This aggression may even be facilitated by the sense that it is "his" child toward whom she feels aggressive.

The need for being babied on the part of women may be an important, positively selected trait, for we can recognize its adaptive significance. Women often, in the course of courtship, assume a "baby" role of cuteness and ineptitude. This role functions as a test, as it were, of the male's way of responding to babies in general. If he finds her attractive in this role, if he is provoked by her babyishness to be gentle, fatherly, a gentle man or "gentleman," then he may be successful in his courtship. A difficulty often experienced by women after the birth of the child is the necessity for dropping the baby role in favor of the mother role. Such a change in role for her is facilitated by the male's assuming the father role. Failure of males to assume the role of father on the birth of children is associated with corresponding fail-

[36] Deutsch, pp. 45–46.

ures of females to assume the role of mother. The maturation into a parental role for either sex is supported by the corresponding maturation into the parental role by the mate.

The fear of loss of sexual attractiveness and the experience of loss of being babied as contributing factors to the desertion of children are ancient themes, represented, for example, in the historically popular "House Carpenter," or "Demon Lover," ballad:

"We have met, we have met, my pretty fair maid,
  We have met, my love," said he;
"For I've just returned from the salty, salty sea,
  And it's all for the love of thee."

"You could have married a rich king's daughter,
  And a handsome one was she;
But I am married to a house carpenter,
  And a handsome man is he."

"If you will forsake your house carpenter,
  And go along with me,
I'll take you where the grass grows green
  Or to keep me from poverty?

"Oh, don't you see those seven, seven ships,
  All sailing for dry land?
Five hundred and ten brave and jolly men
  Shall be at your command."

She called aloud to her sweet and pretty babe,
  She gave it kisses three,
Saying, "Stay at home, my sweet and pretty babe,
  Keep your father's company."

He dressed her up in rich array,
  Most beautiful to behold,
And as she walked the city streets,
  She shone bright as the glittering gold.

They had not been aboard two weeks,
'Twas neither two nor three,
Until this fair lady began to weep,
And she wept most bitterly.

"Oh, is it for my gold you weep,
Or is it for my fee,
Or is it for the house carpenter
That you left across the sea?"

"It's neither for your gold I weep,
Nor is it for your fee,
But alas, it is for that sweet and pretty babe
I left to mourn for me."

They had not been aboard two weeks,
It was neither two nor four,
Until under deck there sprang a leak,
And her mourning was heard no more.[37]

The role of children as inhibitors to free sexual expression is a feature of common experience. Devereux suggests that an important motive for abortion in many cultures is to preserve the beauty of the female and the continued exercise of freedom and irresponsibility.[38] Even Darwin noted that "the trouble experienced by the women in rearing children" and "their consequent loss of beauty" were motives for infanticide.[39] He indicates that motherliness and pregnancy are almost universally regarded as deficits to sexual attractiveness, even in cultures where fertility is especially valued. This reduction in sexual attractiveness may entail the same psychodynamics as those associated with incest

[37] Cited in B. H. Bronson, *The Traditional Tunes of the Child Ballads* (Princeton, N.J.: Princeton University Press, 1966), p. 453.

[38] G. Devereux, *A Study of Abortion in Primitive Societies* (London: T. Yoseloff, 1960), pp. 126–127.

[39] C. Darwin, *The Origin of Species* and *The Descent of Man* (New York: Modern Library, 1936), p. 897.

with one's mother. Every woman runs the risk of the loss of her husband's affection when she becomes a mother, in that the husband carries with him the residues of an incest taboo with respect to his own mother. One study indeed found that pregnancy in the wife is associated with sexual way-wardness in the husband,[40] which may be explained by the arousal of this incest taboo. Vladimir Nabokov's imaginary Lolita,[41] who is physically and in age quite removed from motherhood, or Sebastian Grant's fictional Carmen, Baby,[42] thus become images of sexual attractiveness. *Carmen, Baby* has a telling passage:

The image of her body swollen by pregnancy, the idea of her breasts suckling anything but a passionate lover, the picture of Carmen, poor and tired and tamed by the drab routine of "respectable" living, the fire banked, the gaiety gone, the goddess brought to heel by the stove and the cradle—to tame Carmen would be to destroy everything that was exciting and wonderful about her. She was like a beautiful jungle bird and I wanted love to transform her into a shy brown wren. And when she became the wren, busy with her nest, busy with her fledglings, would I still love her? Would I still want her? When my jungle creature was trapped in the cages of civilization, would she still excite me? I told myself that she would, but I now think that I lied.[43]

Hostility toward children is generally associated with two age-maturity distortions. First, the adult may ascribe to himself the role of a person younger than he actually is. Second, he may ascribe to the child a maturity beyond the child's years. Zilboorg cites the case of a man who attempted

[40] A. A. Hartman and R. C. Nicolay, "Sexually Deviant Behavior in Expectant Fathers," *Journal of Abnormal Psychology,* 1966, *71,* 232.
[41] V. Nabokov, *Lolita* (New York: Putnam's, 1958).
[42] S. Grant, *Carmen, Baby* (New York: Universal, 1968).
[43] Grant, p. 75.

to commit suicide after the death of one of his children and after he had betrayed his own unconscious wish to himself by inadvertently saying, "One mouth less to feed." Discussing his motivation, Zilboorg says: "When we inquire into the deeper strata of, and motivations for, his sadism, we shall find a rather intricate and subtle mechanism; his children he treated as rivals; they were so many 'mouths' which competed with him, not as if he were the father of his children, but the brother of so many little brothers whom he hated. One is impressed by the infantile nature of the man's reactions; he seems to have remained all his life in the throes of the old infantile family conflict even at the age of thirty-six and at the official level of a *pater familias*."[44]

Persons who abuse children also characteristically overestimate and misperceive the maturity of the child.[45] Richard Galdston observes that "in the extremity of their ambivalence these parents perceive the child they assault as a hostile, persecutory adult." They speak of the child "as if he were an adult with all the adult's capacity for deliberate, purposeful, and organized behavior."[46] One group of observers indicated that some of the women who abused male children could do it "because they simply saw the child unrealistically as a grown man."[47] The attribution of sexual precocity may also be present. A mother of a three-year-old daughter whom she had victimized said: "Look at her give

[44] G. Zilboorg, "Depressive Reactions Related to Parenthood," *American Journal of Psychiatry*, 1931, *10*, 930.

[45] See M. G. Morris and R. W. Gould, *Role Reversal: A Concept in Dealing with the Neglected/Battered-Child Syndrome* (New York: Child Welfare League of America, 1963).

[46] R. Galdston, "Observations on Children Who Have Been Physically Abused and Their Parents," *American Journal of Psychiatry*, 1965, *122*, 442.

[47] H. M. Feinstein, N. Paul, and P. Esmiol, "Group Therapy for Mothers with Infanticidal Impulses," *American Journal of Psychiatry*, 1964, *120*, 883.

101

you the eye! That's how she picks up men—she's a regular sexpot."[48]

The attribution of maturity is at least a partial license to abuse the child who is threatening the adult. In addition, it is probably also true that the child is perceived by the parent as in some way his own parent who abused him in his childhood.[49] The trend in times past to conceive of the child as a small adult, dressing the child in clothing designed principally for the life of an adult, and the doctrine that children are born in depravity may be ideological reflections of such psychodynamic patterns. Philippe Aries[50] has indicated that the very idea of childhood as a life period did not arise until modern times is relatively novel in history. Bruno Bettelheim[51] has properly interpreted the historical lack of an idea of childhood as an indication of the limited maturity of the adults of an earlier period of history.

Steele and Pollock, who have treated child-abusing parents, suggest that the frustrated dependency needs of parents are critical in triggering abusive responses. The parents resent the dependency of their children because they themselves lack satisfaction of these needs. They themselves would be babied. Speaking of their treatment of these parents, Steele and Pollock comment:

Although protection of the infant is a main goal, direct interest in the infant should be avoided by the therapist, paradoxical as this may seem. Attention should be focused almost exclusively on the parent. The rationale for this lies in the fact that paying attention to the baby leaves the parent back

[48] Galdston, p. 442.

[49] I. Kaufman, "Psychiatric Implications of Physical Abuse of Children," in *Protecting the Battered Child* (Denver: American Humane Association, 1962), pp. 17–22.

[50] P. Aries, *Centuries of Childhood* (New York: Knopf, 1962).

[51] B. Bettelheim, *The Children of the Dream* (New York: Macmillan, 1969), p. 53.

in the old nightmarish feeling of nobody listening to his needs, thereby reinforcing his hopelessness and lack of trust. Probably our most basic tenet in treatment has been to get the parent to look to us to find out how to get his needs filled, rather than to the infant for satisfaction. If this can be accomplished to even a moderate degree, there is less demand on the baby, less parental frustration, and the baby is essentially safe.[52]

The tendency to abuse the child is related to the enhancement of the abuser's image of himself as being grown-up and adequate. The mechanism is similar to one which has been identified in criminal behavior: "Aggressive action is a reactive state which results from a sense of passivity."[53]

As I have indicated, the very helplessness of the child may be the stimulus that evokes abuse, although helplessness may also evoke care-taking. We should not be surprised to find that the helplessness which elicits care and succor should equally be the stimulus for abuse and infanticide. Having a single stimulus for quite opposite reactions is not an infrequent phenomenon. A frightening stimulus may produce flight in one instance and a "freeze" in another. A hostile gesture may be the stimulus either for an intense aggressive assault or for passivity, submission, or indifference. In the same way the negative reaction against the child, the impulse toward infanticide, may work in a paradoxical way to protect the child by dynamically producing a reaction against the infanticidal impulse. The infanticidal impulse may cause the parent to invest more energy than he would otherwise in the care of the child. The psychological opposite to hate is not so much love as it is indifference. Hate and love coexist in opposition to indifference The psycho-

---

[52] B. F. Steele and C. B. Pollock, "A Psychiatric Study of Parents Who Abuse Infants and Small Children," in Helfer and Kempe, p. 140.

[53] L. Bender and F. J. Curran, "Children and Adolescents Who Kill," *Journal of Criminal Psychopathology*, 1940, *1*, 320.

analyst Rado suggests this functional significance of the infanticidal impulse in child care. He recites some observations of a woman on a beach and her five-year-old child.
"Whatever she was doing, [this woman] glanced up anxiously
every few minutes, sought her boy with a look of concern,
and if she could not immediately detect his whereabouts, began to call in a despairing manner, 'Ma-a-a-ssimo, Ma-a-a-
ssimo.' " Rado's speculation is that this behavior is "repression by means of reaction-formation," that the woman had
intense aggressive impulses toward the child, and that she
converted the internal, albeit unconscious, perception of the
impulse to an external perception of danger to the child.[54]
It is obvious that the mother behaved as if her boy, when
playing on the beach, were threatened with some unknown
dangers and must be shielded with the utmost caution from
some harm. . . . She displaced the evil spirits, which she
detected, from within herself to the outside world, scenting
dangers and menaces everywhere."[55] The result of such a
mechanism is that the child is, in truth, protected from
drowning and the like. And, perhaps, the positive function
of the infanticidal impulse is the paradoxical manner in
which it can result in the increased longevity of infants and
children.

A commonly cited stimulus for child abuse is "the
child's persistently wet and dirty habits . . . or sometimes
his incessant crying."[56] Babies are naturally helpless, inept,
weak, and irregular in excretion, and their needfulness may
create unpleasantness for others. The child urinates and def-
ecates. He throws up. He cannot feed himself, and when he
tries to, he makes a mess of things. He cries and whimpers
and asks for attention. When he is not given attention, he

[54] S. Rado, "An Anxious Mother: A Contribution to the Analysis of
the Ego," *International Journal of Psychoanalysis,* 1928, *9,* 219.

[55] Rado, p. 220.

[56] M. Blumberg, "When Parents Hit Out," *Twentieth Century,*
1964–1965, *173,* 43.

may even develop "neurotic" mechanisms to irritate others into giving him the attention he is not otherwise able to get. Describing the fathers of children who were killed by them, one investigator indicates that the rages against the children were triggered by "prolonged and repeated crying episodes, defecation in their clothing, persistent harassment and other temper-abrading and eroding activities" on the part of the children.[57] Galdston describes a mother who beat ten-month-old son because she experienced his cries as "so demanding."[58] Howard M. Feinstein and his colleagues describe another mother: "One night she awoke to feed her screaming hungry baby. The feeding didn't stop the baby from crying and she became furious. 'I could have killed him,' she said."[59] In an extremely sensitive piece of fictional writing, describing a most plausible context for infanticide, John Updike represents the immmediate stimulus as the defecation of the child. Believing that her husband has again deserted her, "Janice . . . runs to the crib and nightmarishly finds it smeared with orange mess. 'Damn you, damn you,' she moans to Rebecca and lifts the little filthy thing out and wonders where to carry her. She takes her to the armchair and biting her lips unpins the diaper. 'You little pig,' she murmurs." Then the baby drowns in her hands in an overfilled bathtub, "and she knows, knows . . . that the worst thing that has ever happened to any woman in the world has happened to her."[60]

The crying and the helplessness of the child are also evocative of the past, a past which has been buried but is not quite dead, in the mind of the adult. That past can be elicited by a smell or a sound or the sight of a raindrop on

[57] L. Adelson, "Slaughter of the Innocents," *New England Journal of Medicine*, 1961, *264*, 1346.

[58] Galdston, p. 442.

[59] Feinstein, Paul, and Esmiol, p. 883.

[60] J. Updike, *Rabbit, Run* (New York: Knopf, 1960), pp. 262, 264.

105

the pane. And if that past is odious and filled with the dread of being killed and the sense of helplessness and crying and whimpering, then one is easily moved to destroy whatever it is that elicits it. Paradoxically, in this attempt to keep the past dead, it emerges again and again in the behavior of the child, to be ended with the total destruction of the child.

The process we may assume to exist is something as follows: The crying of the baby or other signs of helplessness evoke corresponding and sympathetic responses in the adult. However, the cry of the baby may be most unsettling and bring the parent to a point where he would kill the baby, with the literal killing being the acting out of the inward repression of childhood memories. In some way the child's helplessness acts as a reminder of the old and repressed passivity and helplessness experienced in childhood. The parent wants to immunize himself against those reminders; he wants to be nonhelpless. Thus, he arrogates to himself complete power over the life of another, the child. This sense of power makes his own helplessness less.

Some ideological support for this theory is found in the general Western belief, expressed in some of the offshoots of Calvinism, that one who is needful should be punished for it. This belief was rationalized by the social Darwinistic movement, which tended to regard care for the needy as somehow interfering with the overweening cosmic plan to weed out the unfit and thus make the species superior.

FIVE

The Sins of the Fathers

The significance of child abuse for population control is not exhausted by direct increased mortality. Child abuse has further psychological consequences among those who have been victimized—consequences which function as further population checks. Prior to birth, population may be controlled by continence, contraception, and abortion, and following birth, by infanticide, which is direct, or by cumulative injury. That victims of child abuse survive does not mean that the population-controlling function of child abuse has been exhausted. The effects may continue for several generations, a bitter confirmation of the biblical assertion that the iniquities of the fathers are visited upon the children even unto the third and fourth generations.[1]

[1] Exod. 20:5, 34:7; Num. 14:18; and Deut. 5:9.

Slaughter of the Innocents

ABUSED CHILDREN DIE MORE READILY

One of the principal effects of child abuse on a child is to create traits which lead to death in ways other than from direct injury. R. Spitz discovered that children in foundling homes, where they are fed, bathed, and so on, but not held, talked to, and bounced as normal children would be, have a substantially higher death rate than would be expected under the circumstances.[2] In the extreme, the totally neglected (although fed and minimally cared for) child tends to develop a disease called marasmus, which is an apathy that quickly leads to death. Sandor Ferenczi, a psychoanalyst, discusses the psychodynamics of such deferential dying in a paper entitled "The Unwelcome Child and His Death-Instinct." These unwelcome guests, "children who are received in a harsh and disagreeable way, die easily and willingly. Either they use one of the many proffered organic possibilities for a quick exit, or if they escape this fate, they keep a streak of pessimism and of aversion to life."[3]

The clinical literature on a variety of disturbances of children, both physical and emotional, amply indicates the significance in the creation of these disturbances of the withdrawal of affection from children. As one practitioner puts it: "Where [children] find hate and violently destructive feelings, they invariably blame themselves and conclude that they neither deserve love nor life"[4] and develop illnesses. The communication of hostility to children may be both subtle and direct. Martin Lakin made a careful study of twenty mothers of excessively crying, colicky infants, as judged by pediatricians. These twenty mothers were compared with a

[2] R. Spitz, *The First Year of Life* (New York: International Universities, 1965).

[3] S. Ferenczi, "The Unwelcome Child and His Death-Instinct," *International Journal of Psychoanalysis,* 1929, *10,* 127.

[4] D. Bloch, "Feelings That Kill," *Psychoanalytic Review,* 1965, *52,* 52.

108

group of twenty mothers whose children were judged to be normal. Lakin found that "mothers of colicky infants show greater tentativeness, insecurity, and lack of facility in the carrying out of mothering functions than do mothers of control norms infants. The attitude is often one of helpless contemplation of the infant or of wavering between several courses of action rather than prompt and efficacious meeting of the infant's needs."[5]

ABUSED CHILDREN ARE UNLOVABLE

Furthermore, children who are abused tend to develop characteristics which make them even more unlovable. The well taken care of child attracts positive responses. The child who is abused and neglected becomes ugly in appearance and behavior and invites further abuse and neglect. Abused children develop such traits as fear of being alone, continued whimpering, shyness, fear of novel situations of any kind, hypersensitiveness to pain, overreactiveness to hostility, depression, hyperactivity, destructiveness, fear of engaging in any action at all even to help themselves, blocking of external manifestations of inner life, and decreased appetite. Oliver S. English and G. H. Pearson[6] comment: "The human being whose needs are not met when he comes into the world, who is an unwelcome addition to the family, who is neglected and who lives in an environment that is indifferent and cold toward him will develop hostility, resentment, hate, pessimism—all of which make it very difficult for him to function." The very stifling of development prolongs the helplessness of the child, which continues to be the provocation for further assault or neglect.

[5] M. Lakin, *An Investigation of Personality Characteristics of Mothers of Excessively Crying (Colicky) Infants,* unpublished thesis, University of Chicago, 1955.

[6] O. S. English and G. H. Pearson, *Emotional Problems of Living* (3rd ed.) (New York: Norton, 1963), p. 6.

Even hospital personnel may tend to neglect victims of abuse. Thus, one investigator, discussing victimized children, observes:

We began discovering that the child in the bed farthest from the nurse's station was sometimes a child that fitted into this syndrome. . . . Somehow these children establish the same relationship to the nurses [as to their parents]. When you walk through the ward you can judge by the number of toys on beds; these children have less toys. You can count the pictures in their rooms. Somehow the response they're getting from the nurse is less warm.[7]

It is sometimes a problem to get hospital personnel to care for child abuse victims properly, to overcome their aversions to them. Discussing hospital treatment, Galdston indicates: "Gradually the child moves from total passivity to increasingly active behavior. It is at this stage that a change in personnel occasionally is indicated. Often the children are unappealing, and their early activity may be offensive."[8] Placement of these children is difficult for these reasons. Serapio R. Zalba,[9] in discussing the matter of placing children away from their parents to protect them for their physical safety, indicates the characteristic unlovability: "Because of the abuse he has experienced he may also have emotional and behavioral disorders (e.g., bed-wetting, truanting, fire-setting, or withdrawing) that make him extremely hard to place in foster home care. . . . Keeping him in placement may require moving him as he aborts a number of placements." It is certainly the case, as David Gil[10] points out,

---

[7] K. Bain and others, "Child Abuse and Injury," *Military Medicine*, 1965, *130*, 750, 752.

[8] R. Galdston, "Observations on Children Who Have Been Physically Abused and Their Parents," *American Journal of Psychiatry*, 1965, *122*, 441.

[9] S. R. Zalba, "The Abused Child. I. A Summary of the Problem," *Social Work*, 1966, *4*, 9.

[10] D. G. Gil, "A Nationwide Epidemiologic Study on Child Abuse—

"that some children may be more provocative than others in their behavior toward adults and that such children may play a contributing role in their own physical abuse." The contribution to unlovability from being unloved must be part of the equation.

The simple consequence is that the victimized child has been made unattractive in a way which works against his receiving the kind of love and attention which will make him thrive in the future. The abuse of a child creates a child who invites abuse. The abused child is truly the spoiled child, more than any overindulged child could be. The spoiled child in the latter sense may tend to make excessive demands upon life, but the former has been made unfit for receiving love.

DERANGEMENT OF SEXUALITY

Perhaps one of the most significant consequences of child abuse with respect to population is that it leads to the derangement of his adult sexuality in a direction away from full procreativity. At the very least, and in fulfillment of commonly held ideals, the judicious use of punishment in the rearing of children makes them moral in the sense of inhibiting sexual expression. Thus, even the mildest forms of punishment are in this sense population-controlling.

But this effect has profound roots in the human condition. Two facts need to be considered together. First, trauma deranges the development of sexuality. Second, virtually every derangement of normal sexuality reduces the likelihood that children will be created. No form of sexual activity outside of heterosexual coitus leads to reproduction. Practices such as masturbation, homosexuality, and sexual contacts with animals are certainly "contraceptive," as are voyeurism, exhibitionism, sadism, masochism, and oral and

Progress Report." Presented at the National Conference on Social Welfare, Chicago, June 1966.

anal sexual activity. Prostitution functions as a brake on population as any form of polyandry does. Even the channeling of libido to assaultive sexual relations on female children is population-controlling in that the likelihood of a prepubertal girl's becoming pregnant is small, the likelihood of survival of the child if she does become pregnant is small, and the creation of a life-long aversion to sexuality in the victim reduces the likelihood of later pregnancy. If we take the relative frequencies of sexually deviant behavior found by Alfred C. Kinsey as even reasonably representative, it seems that he was studying some of the main ways of restricting population in the contemporary world. The frightening possibility is that Kinsey's observations may also bespeak equally widespread child abuse practices which created such large relative frequencies of sexual deviation.

One of the most important conclusions to be extracted from the researches of Freud, Richard von Krafft-Ebing, and others who have studied sexual deviants is that traumatic experiences in childhood are closely linked with sexual deviations in adulthood. Freud conceived of the paradigmatic form of offense that a person may engage in as sexual and the paradigmatic form of punishment as castration, which suggests drastic removal of procreative capability. Freud also recognized that the fantasy of "a child is being beaten" has as its meaning quite specifically that beating of the body or any part is experienced unconsciously as beating of the genitalia.[11] Ferenczi[12] observes that frigidity and impotence are characteristic of unwelcome children. And Harry F. Harlow[13] observes that monkeys with restricted mothering grow up with a markedly reduced tendency to engage in copulation.

That the aim of child abuse, in a biological sense, is

[11] S. Freud, *Collected Papers*, Vol. 3, J. Strachey (Ed.) (London: Hogarth, 1950), p. 494. And Vol. 5, 1952, p. 193.

[12] Ferenczi, pp. 149–154.

[13] H. F. Harlow, "The Heterosexual Affectional System in Monkeys," *American Psychologist*, 1962, *17*, 1–9.

to reduce the likelihood that the child will procreate when he becomes an adult is also suggested by the observation that "children have always been the victims of mutilation practices, the most common site for mutilation being the sex organs,"[14] often with the parent feeling that he is engaging in legitimate punishment for sexual manifestations in the child.

The buttocks are the locus for the induction of pain in a child. We are familiar with the argument that it is a "safe" locus for spanking. However, the anal region is also the major erotic zone at precisely the time at which the child is likely to be beaten there. Thus, it is aptly chosen to achieve the result of deranged sexuality in adulthood, especially if there is any validity in the psychoanalytic observation that the child, albeit unconsciously, interprets punishment generally as punishment for sexual impulse and expression.

To take a more general view, maturation includes the maturation of sexuality. Mature sexuality is a condition in which lust has developed to include love, love for a mature person of the opposite sex has developed to include love for children, and love for children has developed to include conscientious care for them. Progress in maturation is retarded by traumatic experiences. Trauma leads to the arrest of psychosexual development at lower stages of development and sometimes even leads to regression to still less mature levels.

If the individual is fortunate enough to grow into adulthood in accordance with his potentialities, his adulthood is characterized by what psychoanalysts call genitalization and what Erikson calls "generativity." As Zilboorg puts it in discussing the maturation into parenthood, "We know from psychoanalytical experience that man reaches the adult genital level of development very gradually and that

[14] R. E. Helfer and C. H. Kempe (Eds.), *The Battered Child* (Chicago: Chicago University Press, 1968), p. 5.

113

the path of this development is covered with many roughnesses."[15] According to Erikson, "Generativity . . . is primarily the concern in establishing and guiding the next generation. . . . The ability to lose oneself in the meeting of bodies and minds leads to a gradual expansion of ego interests and to a libidinal investment in that which is being generated. Generativity thus is an essential stage on the psychosexual as well as on the psychosocial schedule. . . . Some . . . parents suffer, it seems, from a retardation of the ability to develop this stage." These parents, according to Erikson, are "in the lack of some faith, some 'belief in the species,' which would make a child appear to be a welcome trust of the community."[16]

ABUSED CHILDREN TEND TO BECOME CHILD ABUSERS

If the person who has been abused in childhood becomes the parent of a child, the likelihood of a repetition of abusive practice is great. Here we have a relentless mechanism which continues until the aim of population reduction is achieved, until the line of child abusers is wiped out. One of the greatest ironies of evolution is that insofar as the trait with which we are concerned is natural and genetically carried, it must be carried precisely by those in whom it manifests itself least, that is, by those who reproduce effectively and who rear children effectively. The lines of child abusers must have been repeatedly wiped out in the long history of evolution, yet the trait has evidently been positively selected.

This observation leads to the suggestion that libido is the engine not so much of reproduction but more generally of population control. The energy of libido may serve the

[15] G. Zilboorg, "Depressive Reactions Related to Parenthood," *American Journal of Psychiatry*, 1931, *10*, 933.
[16] E. Erikson, *Childhood and Society* (New York: Norton, 1963), p. 267.

whole continuum from aggression, sadism, child abuse, and infanticide to loving, nurturing, and caring for children. Even the physiology of anger and the physiology of sexual arousal are virtually the same.[17] The ease with which that libido may be deflected is more than amply documented by the thousands of pages of the psychological literature on perversions. Insofar as conditions are experienced as dire, libido serves aggression and the like. The urge to give sexual pleasure is easily changed to the urge to inflict pain. The urges to love and be loved are easily changed into actions of hate and into actions that make one hated. Those who experience trauma in childhood tend to traumatize the young and to perpetuate the deflection of libido, with the result being to make human beings more rare.

Persons who engage in violence tend to have been victims of violence.[18] One study found that "remorseless physical brutality at the hands of the parents had been a constant experience" for first-degree murderers in their childhoods.[19] Every time a child is punished by the use of violence he is being taught that the use of violence is a proper mode of behavior. Violence becomes what superego figures do. It is impossible to use corporal punishment on a child without simultaneously teaching that the deliberate infliction of pain as a form of persuasion and as a means of gaining ascendancy over others is legitimate. The child who is witness to adult violence also quite rightly asks himself why he may not use violence in order to make other people behave in accordance with his wishes. The answer he comes

---

[17] A. C. Kinsey and others, *Sexual Behavior in the Human Female* (Philadelphia: Saunders, 1953), p. 705.

[18] G. M. Duncan, S. H. Frazier, E. M. Litin, A. M. Johnson, and A. J. Barron, "Etiological Factors in First-Degree Murder," *Journal of the American Medical Association*, 1958, *168*, 1755–1758. Also, S. M. Nurse, "Familial Patterns of Parents Who Abuse Their Children," *Smith College Studies in Social Work*, 1964, *35*, 11–25.

[19] G. C. Curtis, "Violence Breeds Violence—Perhaps?" *American Journal of Psychiatry*, 1963, *120*, 386–387.

to is simply that he does not have sufficient physical and social might to inflict pain on others without their retaliating. All that he lacks is power. And as soon as he gets it, he takes it as right that he should use it. Thus, he uses violence on the next generation of children, and so on.

Because child abuse victims learn to abuse children in this manner quite directly, they are filled with a sense of the moral righteousness of what they are doing. The internal injunction in an abusing parent has a kind of moral imperative associated with it which is hard to match. His sense of the righteousness and justice of the act derives from the fact that he himself was so punished in his childhood, and developing the sense that such punishment is legitimate and even righteous was the only way in which he could accept it. One of the greatest obstacles in dealing with a child-abusing parent is this feeling that the actions were justified. Psychologically he has a license from the superego to abuse his child, which is irrevocable, handed down to him at the time he was abused by his original superego figure.

Simple imitation is a factor. Patterns of child-rearing appear to be based on the care received as a child. Zalba says that "if children remain in homes where there is repeated abuse, they are likely to internalize the behavioral models to which they are exposed." He quotes Beatrice Simcox Reiner and Irving Kaufman on this: "Having experienced loss of love or inconsistent care themselves, they are unable as adults to provide a mature and consistent type of parental care for their children but pass on these elements to them. . . . Such parents have a tendency to subject their own children to similar losses and to experiences that will engender the same attitudes."[20]

Lakin, in the study already cited, found that mothers of colicky, crying infants displayed much greater tension and hostility with respect to their own mothers than did the

[20] Zalba, p. 9. 1966

mothers of the children who were normal. The mothers of colicky infants carried "resentment at the lack of support and the greater emotional distance" they had experienced in their childhoods.

The word *bastard* is interesting from this point of view. The word literally means a person whose birth is illegitimate, the offspring of a mother not married, a person who has no claim upon a specific father for support and care. But bastard also means that the person is evil, mean, and unlovable. Bastard in the first sense suggests that the child is likely neglected and abused. Bastard in the second sense means that the person is intrinsically undesirable. These two meanings converge into the one word because the two meanings characteristically converge in fact. Bastards tend to become bastards, and if they breed, they tend to beget bastards in turn. That word is less frequently used by women; but, characteristically, when women use it, they are describing a man who abandons a woman who has become pregnant by him. And she, uttering the word as though it were the ultimate curse, psychologically fuses the bastard growing within her with the father. Her child, abused and neglected as he is likely to be, is truly a bastard in one sense and is likely to become a bastard in the other.

SIX

Toward a Solution

No simple solution to the problem dealt with in this book exists. Yet certainly there appear directions in which we may move. The problem of child abuse is related to the fundamental existential issues of human life and is rooted in man's psychobiological nature. The impulse toward child abuse may be, at least latently, ubiquitous. I have suggested that it may be part of man's basic evolutionary equipment for keeping population under control relative to the resources available for sustaining human life. But if it is natural, it is so in the sense that seeking food, building shelter, and fashioning clothing against the cold are natural. Unfortunately, in this natural occurrence it is ugly and evil.

Culture, however, is also natural to man. Fortunately

culture may, to a fairly high degree, be fashioned to suit circumstances. We must look to the possibility of cultural change for finding the solutions to the problem of child abuse. With all the complexities involved and all the limitations of oversimplified formulations, it yet appears that the main cause of child abuse is the burdensomeness of children. Many factors contribute to variation in the experience of burdensomeness, and many factors counterbalance it on the other side. Yet that word will do well for summarizing the main thought of this book. From the viewpoint of evolutionary theory the burdensomeness depends on the discrepancy between the demands by people on the resources for living and the availability of resources.

How do we then move toward the cultural rectification of the situation? I believe that if the following two articles from the *Universal Declaration of Human Rights,* declared by the General Assembly of the United Nations in 1949, could become universal in man's consciousness, law, and custom, then substantial progress could be made in coping with the problem of child abuse:

Article 5. *No one shall be subjected to torture or to cruel, inhuman, or degrading treatment or punishment.*

Article 25. *(1) Everyone has the right to a standard of living adequate for the health and well-being of himself and of his family, including food, clothing, housing, and medical care and necessary social services, and the right to security in the event of unemployment, sickness, disability, widowhood, old age, or other lack of livelihood in circumstances beyond his control. (2) Motherhood and childhood are entitled to special care and assistance. All children, whether born in or out of wedlock, shall enjoy the same social protection.*

Article 5 should, in light of the evidence of child abuse, be interpreted to include children. There is, unfortunately, widespread acceptance of the belief that it is proper to win obedience and social compliance through the use of force and violence; and somehow, by chains of reasoning, emotional associations, and tradition, it is felt that in the microcosm of child-rearing it is equally proper to use force and violence to obtain obedience and social compliance. One can only speculate on the relationship between child-rearing practices and international and civil war. Yet, perhaps an important step that may yet be taken in the remainder of this century is the honoring of Article 5 for children as well as for adults.

Article 25 (2) implicitly recognizes that the welfare of society is contingent on the quality of human beings that the society raises to adulthood. If, as has been made so abundantly clear, the child is truly the father of the man and if those who have been the recipients of love and care are likely, in turn, to render love and care to others, then the whole society becomes the beneficiary when children are loved and cared for. A society which cares for its children and thus also teaches those children to care for their children in turn thrives indefinitely. A society which neglects or abuses its children exists precariously. Indeed, if, as some economists have cogently argued, the quality of human beings is becoming increasingly important for the well-being of the total society, the rearing of quality human beings may be society's most important task.[1]

Some enterprises in society require support through taxation rather than through individual expenditure of resources. Though individuals may profit in different degrees, the common good is best served when these enterprises receive public support. A conspicuous example is that of roads. Roads certainly benefit the immediate user. Yet it is to the greater advantage of all that roads be publicly supported

[1] T. W. Schultz (Ed.), *Investment in Human Beings,* supplement to *Journal of Political Economy,* October 1962.

rather than being supported by the direct user. The common wisdom of mankind has thus provided that, except in some special instances, the support of roads by tolls is less desirable than the support of roads by taxation.

It is equally on the side of wisdom that the society move quickly toward the support by taxation of the mother-child unit in the spirit of the second part of Article 25, rendering special care and assistance wherever needed. This change would go a long way toward the satisfaction of dependency needs, the frustration of which is a major factor in child abuse. This solution to the general problem is far better than any forced breach of the mother-child unit. The latter may be necessary in that small percentage of child abuse cases in which there is unambiguous and frank psychosis in the parent. However, in most cases what is required is the rendering of literal support "including food, clothing, housing, and medical care and necessary social services, and the right to security . . ."

We must always remember that children become the adult members of the society and must share the planet with each other. If all children are not properly provided for, then all the adults who were once children, whether they themselves were or were not properly provided for as children, bear the consequences of it.

Index

A

Abattoir, 72
ABIRAM, 29
Abolitionist movement, 47
Abortion, 44, 80, 91, 107
ABRAHAM, 16, 27, 28, 71
Abuses enumerated, 4
ADAM, 70
Adaptation, individual versus group, 96
ADELSON, L., 26, 105
ADLER, A., 58
AHAZ, 29
Alice in Wonderland, 71
Amphidroma ceremony, 32
Ancient Tahiti, 30
Anger, 92, 115
Anti-Semitism, 34
APTEKAR, H., 56
ARIES, P., 102

ARISTOTLE, 31
Assault, sexual, 112
Attention, demand for stimulus, 104–105

B

Baba Yaga, 66, 67
Baby farms, 67
"Baby" role, 97–98
Baby's Hospital, 50
BAIN, K., 91, 110
BAKAN, D., 58, 95
Baptism, 32, 33
Barleycorn, John, 34, 35
Barnakarl, 33
BARRON, A. J., 115
Bastard, meanings of, 116
Bear, 71
Before Thy Heart Had Learn'd, 86
Belsen, 7
Ben Casey, 45

Index

124

Index

127

Index